To Dorothy,
My parents and family,
with special thanks
to all the wonderful people who have
touched my life and work in so many ways.

AN APPLAUSE ORIGINAL

TAKE IT PERSONALLY:
On the Art and Process of Personal Acting
by Gordon Phillips

Copyright © 2000 by Gordon Phillips
ISBN 1-55783-390-7

Library of Congress Cataloging-in-Publication Data

Library of Congress Catalog Card Number: 99-65409

British Library Cataloging-in-Publication Data
A catalog record for this book is available from the British Library.

APPLAUSE BOOKS

1841 Broadway	Combined Book Services Ltd.
Suite 1100	Units I/K Paddock Wood Dist. Ctr.
New York, NY 10023	Paddock Wood,
Phone (212) 765-7880	Tonbridge Kent TN12 6UU
Fax: (212) 765-7875	Phone 0189 283-7171
	Fax 0189 283-7272

PRINTED IN CANADA

TAKE IT
PERSONALLY

GORDON PHILLIPS

THE APPLAUSE ACTING SERIES

ACTING IN FILM by Michael Caine

ACTING IN RESTORATION COMEDY
 by Simon Callow

ACTING WITH SHAKESPEARE: The Comedies
 by Janet Suzman

THE ACTOR'S EYE: Seeing and Being Seen
 by David Downs

THE ACTOR AND THE TEXT by Cicely Berry

ACCIDENTALLY ON PURPOSE by John Strasberg

THE CRAFTSMEN OF DIONYSUS by Jerome Rockwood

CREATING A CHARACTER by Moni Yakim

DIRECTING THE ACTION by Charles Marowitz

DUO! The Best Scenes for the 90s

FUNDAMENTAL ACTING: by Paul Kuritz

THE MONOLOGUE WORKSHOP by Jack Poggi

ONE ON ONE: Best Monologues for the 90s (Men&Women)

ON SINGING ONSTAGE by David Craig

**THE OTHER WAY: An Alternative Approach to Acting &
 Directing by Charles Marowitz**

A PERFORMER PREPARES by David Craig

SHAKESCENES: Shakespeare for Two
 Edited by John Russell Brown

SOLILOQUY! The Shakespeare Monologues (Men & Women)

SOLO! The Best Monologues of the 80s (Men & Women)

SPEAK WITH DISTINCTION by Edith Skinner
 Edited by Lilene Mansell and Timothy Monich
 90-minute audiotape also available

STANISLAVSKI REVEALED by Sonia Moore

STYLE: Acting in High Comedy by Maria Aitken

THE VOCAL VISION
 edited by Marian Hampton and Barbara Acker

CONTENTS

PART II - USING THE TOOLS IN A ROLE

NOTE

Although not the intital intent, this book in its present form could be used to teach a complete course in acting. Use each tool and its supporting exercises as an outline for individual lessons, supplemented at your discretion

INTRODUCTION

My primary purpose in writing this book is to take the mystery out of good acting, to present a clear, practical set of organic "craft tools" that allow the actor to perform any style of material in any media with confidence. The primary tool of acting is very familiar and accessible to you – your own being! Acting is the art you make out of yourself.

I taught acting for Lee Strasberg for seven years. He'd say, "We call what I do 'The Method' and not the Stanislavsky 'System' because I may do things he wouldn't approve of." Then, with a twinkle in his eye, he'd add, "And at the same time, I want to get credit for the improvements I've made." For the same reasons, I call what I do "The Process."

The Process is acting as a way of BEING. There's no style of acting or media that the Process doesn't address.

We begin with a general overview some qualities possessed by the most exciting actors, then proceed with the practical acting tools needed to make these qualities work for you.

A GUIDE TO THE ACTOR'S TOOLBOX
QUALITIES POSSESSED BY EXCITING
ACTORS THAT CAN WORK FOR YOU

TO REACH FOR HIGHER ACTING, REACH FOR THE "HIGHER SELF"

PRESCRIPTION: Read once a day

TRANSFORM THE IMAGINARY INTO THE REAL

You need the childlike ability to believe the imaginary is real, to enter, on cue, into and live fully within the fantasy world of a play or film as an imaginary character. (Tools #1, 2, 3 . . . and most of the tools that follow.)

PRIVACY ON THE SET OR IN FRONT OF AN AUDIENCE OR CAMERA

Reveal the private, quirky, personal behaviors that normal-ly happen only when we're totally alone. Capture those pri-vate individualized traits that make us – and the character– unique and special. (Tools #1, 2, 3, and 10.)

MAKE PERSONAL THE IMPERSONAL SCRIPT

The written script is not personal to the actor before he

works on it. For the character, the script is very personal. The actor's job is to make the impersonal script as personal to himself as it is to his character. Apply your inner life to the given circumstances of the play. (Tools #5 and 6.)

REVEAL THE WHOLENESS OF WHO WE ARE

Be willing to expose your dark side through the character, as well as the light side. The artist-actor shows all sides of herself and her character, sometimes simultaneously. The dark, shadow sides are generally the most dramatic and interesting. Various shadings give depth and contrast. (Tools #5, 10, 12, 13.)

LIVE IN THE MOMENT

Don't anticipate; have no expectations. Nothing should be overly fixed or rigid. Stay spontaneous and open. Trust your instincts and intuition. (Tools #8, 10, 14.)

TRULY EXPRESS ON THE OUTSIDE ALL THAT'S GOING ON INSIDE YOU AND THE CHARACTER

Wear your heart (and therefore, your character's heart) on your sleeve. Even your inner thoughts can be read by an audience or camera. The best actor is transparent. Thoughts should be at least as loud as words, especially in film. (Tools #5, 10, 12, 13.)

KEEP A STRONG INNER SUBTEXT ALIVE

The text is the tip of the iceberg for the actor; the subtext the other seven-eighths. What's going on underneath the script? The text is what the playwright writes. The subtext is what the actor "writes." (Tools #5, 7, 12, 13, 14.)

FOCUS TOTALLY ON ACCOMPLISHING YOUR GOAL

Be driven and consumed by the need to obtain an objective as a character, and in your career. Be almost obsessive. (Part 1 of Tool #8.)

SURPRISE AN AUDIENCE

Let the audience think everything's going the way they expect, and then *WHAM!*, do something completely unexpected. (Tool #14.)

CARRY AN AIR OF MYSTERY

While exposing everything, project a feeling there's an even more powerful secret that may (or may not) come out at any moment – one that'll blow everyone away. (Tools #13 and 14.)

EXPRESS THE INADEQUACY OF WORDS

Learn to communicate the frustrating feeling that words are inadequate to show the fullness of experience; imply there's so much more underneath. (Speaking out the subtext; Tool #13.)

MAGNETIC PRESENCE.

Project a feeling of electrified energy, an aliveness. This may be a quiet intensity, a radiated warmth, an aura that attracts and is attractive. (See Part 3, #6, on Magnetizing an Audience.)

AN ANIMAL QUALITY

Be unpredictable, instinctual, spontaneous, lithe, relaxed but alert, playful and/or deadly; uncertain, not fully tamed, independent. (Tools #10, 14, 17.)

LIVE CLOSE TO THE EDGE (BUT NEVER OVER IT)

Be willing to go to the limit – fully open, not playing safe but never hurting oneself or others in any way. Have the courage to be different, to be original. (Tools #10, 14.)

SENSUALITY.

Communicate sensual excitement, either intensive or quiet. Be alive and open to all your sensuality, physically vibrant and resonating, uninhibited when called for, all the senses awake and attuned. (Tools #10, 13, 16, 17.)

A SELF-MOCKING SENSE OF HUMOR

Look for the irony in any situation. Take the work seriously but don't take yourself seriously. (Tools #1, 14.)

DRAMATIC CHOICE

When faced with a choice or direction in acting or theatre, always pick the most dramatic. Many actors choose the easier, less dramatic course. Strew the path with as many obstacles as possible. (Part 2 of Tool #8, 10, 14.)

INNER AUTHORITY

Have belief in yourself, feel confident, cooperative yet independent, self-assured. Be accepting and forgiving of yourself and others. (Mastering all the tools.)

POWERFUL CONCENTRATION

Be fully focused, with a strong intensity and involvement in whatever you do; there should be no room for stagefright, which is concentration on self. (Tools #1, 2, 3.)

VITALITY

Have spunk, drive, energy; a sense of humor, aliveness, enthusiasm, positiveness. Pay attention to good nutrition and health habits. (Sports, Physical Exercises, Dance. Tools #3, 10, 17.)

HARD WORK

Go as far as you can, then stretch to test your limits. Work longer, harder, and more intensely than anyone else. (All Tools.)

FEELING WORTHY

Have a quiet belief in yourself. Know you're worthy to have what you want. Feel confident; have a priate feeling you're special, that you deserve to succeed. (Exercise: Tool #1, 8.)

USE YOUR PERSONAL IDIOSYNCRASIES

Display the personal rituals and distinctive ways you behave and perform everyday mannerisms; Mine the peculiar, the personal, and the special acting ore within you. Have a personal style and flair that's yours and your character's. (Tools #10, 13, 14.)

A DIRECT, NON-INTELLECTUAL EXPERIENCE OF REALITY

Have an awareness of the unity and interrelation of all things and events. Avoid all phoneyness. Feel a oneness and wholeness with your character, the other characters, and the play. (Tool #5, 6.)

ACT NATURE, NOT ACTING

The exciting actors are people you enjoy being with, at least for the length of a performance. The really good ones you feel you could be with for a lifetime. They don't have to "act" acting; they naturally possess the qualities of people you like to be with. You can't be more of an actor than you are a human being; you can't give what you don't have. (All the Tools; Magnetizing an Audience, Part 3, #6.)

"DYNAMIC LETHARGY"

On the inside, have a dynamic energy, while outside be relaxed and almost lethargic. (Tools #1, 2, 3, Magnetizing an Audience, Part 3, #6.)

SEEK THE TRUTH OF A SITUATION WITH PASSION

Always welcome the chance to do your best. Find the balanced blend of the real and the ideal. Look for truth with passion and passion with truth. Be as close to the truth as possible at all times. (All Tools.)

A TEASING QUALITY

Give the feeling there's always more, that you're holding back a little. Give the impression, true or not, that if you really let go – look out! (Tools #1, 13, 14, 17.)

WORK THROUGH SHYNESS

Don't let shyness hold you back. Shyness can be an asset. Often, shy people are sensitive and empathetic – good qualities for an actor. A shy person who works to reach her inherent quality of boldness, if needed, is more interesting than an actor who's only bold or only shy. (Tools #10; Part 3, #6.)

COURAGE

There's a fearsome barrier many actors stop short of cross-
ing – personal pain, whether psychological or physical.
Then there are the brave few who have the courage to leap
over it or break through it. The courageous actor offers up
his performance as if it were a ritual self-sacrifice. (All
Tools).

EARLY LESSONS

ACTING HELPS US LIVE OUR UNLIVED LIVES.

When I was a teenager, a friend of mine, Harold Primm, was part of a small dramatic club. He thought his group could help me with my acute shyness. He overcame my strong resistance by agreeing I'd never have to go on the stage. I would work only with the friendly, undermanned backstage crew. Needless to say, a few days before the opening of a short play, *The Ghost of Jerry Bundler*, one of the actors got very sick. One heroic actor, eager for a bigger part, was ready to fill in. Anyone, he declared, could take over his one-line part. They looked around, and their eyes fell on me. "No way," I protested. "You promised." Then Elsie Schmit gave me The Look. Everyone knew I was infatuated with Elsie, since I couldn't keep my eyes off her (when I thought she wasn't looking) and blushed when she noticed. Elsie looked at my red face and said, "Oh, *please*, we need you." I was trapped.

The play concerns a ghost who appears on this old estate every hundred years on the same date. The present owner gives a party to spoof the ridiculous superstition. In the middle of the festivities, the butler backs into the room with a tray full of drinks, turns around and, horrified, announces, "I've seen it! I've seen it! The ghost of Jerry Bundler!" That was my part. Despite my devout wish that some natural disaster would save me, opening night came right on cue. I had rehearsed my one line ten thousand times. Harold

23

arrived at my house a few hours early to personally escort me to the theater. I still went into shock. The stage manager made sure I was in place early. My cue came; she gave me a sharp nudge. On I went. When I backed in and finally turned around with the glasses on the tray tinkling together, my face was ashen and in a trembling voice I uttered, "I saw a ghost." No one doubted it! It may have been the best "acting" I've ever done. Everyone on stage rushed out to see the ghost. I put down my tray of glasses and made my exit.

With my costume still on, I went out the stage door and aimlessly walked the dark streets, tears streaming down my cheeks. The same words repeated in my head. "I DID IT! I DID IT! And I'm still alive!"

The discovery that you could be real in acting excited me and set the tone for the rest of my life in the theater. And this all happened on the first night of my very first play!

The next important discovery came much later, on another first night – the first night of my first Broadway play. That night would also have a significant effect on the rest of my life in the theater. The play was *Marathon '33* by June Havoc, starring Julie Harris.

When the final curtain came down that night, I sat in my dressing room removing my makeup and wondering why I wasn't more excited. After all, I'd made it to BROADWAY! The opening night party had to wait. I lingered until everyone had gone. I went out on the empty stage with its one lonely work light, and stood looking over the empty house expecting the emotions to come. They never did. All I could think was, "You know, it's just another theater!" I actually felt relieved; instead of crying, I laughed. "IT'S ALL THEATER," I thought, "Broadway is just a location." I'd finally realized that I could enjoy theater no matter what the street address, and I have enjoyed it all. I've done most everything possible in theater, film, and TV. I've worked almost every-where, including Europe.

I hope that by the time you finish reading this book, you'll have come to that same thrilling – and humbling – realization. It's all hard, but it's all exciting.

TAKING THE MYSTERY
OUT OF ACTING

The Study of Acting Is the Study of Life.

Included with each of the following tools of acting is a clarifying exercise. Doing the exercises will give you a practical way of understanding the tool more fully. You may choose to read the book straight through the first time and then go back and do the work more thoroughly.

Don't think of the exercises as just technical. Most not only serve as training tools for the actor but can be used directly in production. Perhaps even more importantly the exercises lead to an organic inner technique, a valuable mystical space that's easier for you to experience through the exercises than for me to try to tell you about. Gradually the external work moves inside you, becomes part of you and you own it. Eventually it flows without effort and you can live fully in the immediate moment on stage or screen. You have to earn that glorious moment and there are no short-cuts. Think of the exercises as the solid foundation for the pages that follow.

There's more than one way to approach acting. I know because I've studied most of the ways, the majority first hand, and have found the way laid out in this book to be the most honest, natural, and practical. The closest to the way nature itself works. The Process will not detract from any acting you've already learned or that you do; it will enhance it. As Carlos Castaneda wrote, "find a path with heart and traverse its full length."

You can't learn to act solely from a book. At best, a book can act as a guide, a set of clarifications, a rounding out, and an inspiration.

The greatest advice I can give you is – fall in love with the "process" of acting. Because, really, that's all there is.

If you learn to enjoy the process for itself, you can always be happy, no matter where you wind up.

So, let's get on with The Process!

THE ACTOR'S TOOLBOX

The actor asks, "What does the script require of me and what tools will I use to accomplish that?" Any worker may ask the same question.

A story: A student plumber goes to plumbing school to learn the tools of the trade. He learns to use all manner of sophisticated equipment. His first job upon graduating is to fix a leaking pipe in a basement. Possessed with the fanciest toolbox you can imagine, filled with all kinds of exciting new devices, our enthusiastic hero expertly saws, bends, and contorts his way through the now flooded basement, making a gigantic mess. And all he needed was a single wrench to tighten a joint!

The moral is: learn to use all the tools well, but use only those tools you need for each specific job.

Lesson: There are some craftsmen that become pedestrian, while others, with the exact same tools, become masters, and even a few that find an inner quality that raises their craft to an art. Let's closely explore this quality as we move through the book. Acting is a series of connected processes. Each tool is an individual process, making up, collectively, the whole Process of acting.

The tools of acting are not in themselves acting. The tools are a means, a way.

What follows are the essential tools of the actor.

PART ONE

THE TOOLS OF ACTING

TOOL #1

NEUTRALIZING THE SELF

RELAXATION

Relaxing is not collapsing; its aim is to increase real energy.

The single greatest thief of your natural talent is TENSION – mental, physical, psychological, or spiritual. Experts tell us that the greatest thief of our health is also tension or stress: In the book *Power Through Repose* by Ann P. Call (Little, Brown & Company), she says, "The artist will be bound so long as there is tension in any part of the body." Dr. Deepak Chopra echoes the same statement regarding health and well-being in body, mind, and spirit, in his book *Quantum Healing* (Bantam Books). "Stress is a disease that creates other diseases," according to psychiatrist Ainsley Mears in *Relief Without Drugs.*

If tension is the most powerful enemy of your talent, then its reduction must precede any exercise of that talent. Relaxation is both a training aid and an acting tool. It's a training aid when used before or in conjunction with virtually all exercises, and an acting tool when we use various relaxation techniques to neutralize negative tension that short-circuits our full functioning before or during a performance.

In the Process of acting, you will often "neutralize in order to actualize." Neutralizing is like erasing the slate, cleaning it of the clichéd, the false, the habitual. Neutralizing is a means, not an end. Actualizing means to make real through action.

I prefer a "soft relaxation" technique that you can sneak in to the middle of Act Two, if needed, without anyone in the audience being aware of it.

The technique should eventually be practiced in all positions – standing, sitting, lying down, and while moving all your joints, so that you can learn to relax anywhere, any time you want, in any position. I suggest you start by lying down.

EXERCISES

Relax Mind, Psyche, Spirit, Body

To relax the mind, start to quiet your thoughts. (As the thoughts slow down the body automatically slows down.) As a thought comes in one "door" of the mind, let it go straight out another. Don't hold any thought. Let the thoughts drift by like so many soft clouds, slower and slower. Release all thoughts connected with the past or the future. Slip through the quiet space between thoughts to find the peaceful place beyond thought.

To relax the psyche, think positive thoughts: "I am worthy. I am lovable. I have talent." Counteract your most common fears or negative beliefs with their positive counterparts until you feel yourself letting go.

To relax the spirit, feel at one with the whole universe; feel your connection to everyone and everything. Without you, the universe would not be the same, for it would be missing something important – YOU.

Now, without changing your breathing, be lightly aware of your breath, the inhalations and exhalations, your stomach and chest rising and falling easily. As you inhale, think the sound "hummm" and as you exhale, think the sound "sahhh." Soon you'll be at peace.

To relax the body, and to get out of your head, concentrate on your toes. Be aware of each toe on your left foot, then your right foot. Feel the space between your toes – is it warm, cold, moist, cramped? On the bottom of each foot, notice the crease behind the toes where they join the balls of the feet. Be aware of the balls of the feet. Concentrate on the inside arches and the outside rim, back to the bottom of the heels and the whole bottom of both feet. Be aware of the toenails on the top, then up and around the sides, back to the Achilles tendon, the ankle, and then the whole foot, left and right. With the same awareness go up the leg, lightly concentrating on and relaxing each muscle, joint, bone, and so on. Then achieve the same detailed awareness for the hands and arms. Next, go to the trunk of your body and, starting from the bottom, the space between the genitals and the anus, move up the front and back of the body.

As you move upward, lightly identify all the parts of the body, each vertebra and all the inside organs. Move your concentration slowly up to the shoulders and shoulder blades, front and back of the neck, back of the head, top of the head, scalp and hair, sides of the head, ears, temples, and hinge of jawbone. Move it up to your forehead and all the muscles of the face, nose, cheeks, mouth, eyes, eyebrows, eyelids, letting the pupils rest easily on the bottoms of the eyes.

Check through the whole body, releasing any remaining tension. Put your attention back on your breathing. With each inhalation, think the sound "hummm" and with each exhalation, think the sound "sahhh." You may want to do a visualization – go to an ideal, imaginary place where you once felt perfectly relaxed and with your senses fully alive see it, smell it, hear it, touch the ground beneath you, etc.

When you reach a state of deep relaxation, try lightly touching the right thumb to any part of the index finger next to it. Repeat this thumb and index finger gesture each time you achieve deep relaxation to create an association between feeling relaxed and touching your fingers. Eventually, the touch itself will cue your body to relax. Try it. It works. You may want to use this touch any time you need instant relaxation – in interviews, auditions, while acting, at any stressful time. Relaxation should be a daily practice until it becomes an ingrained habit and you "own" it.

Relaxed Rehearsal

When you're well rehearsed and about to show your finished work, you may wish to invite your co-artists to a "relaxed rehearsal." All the cast members lie on the floor with heads together and legs out like the spokes of a wheel. Do the full rehearsal, or any part of it, with eyes closed in a very relaxed, dreamy manner. Let the unconscious take over. It's a beautiful exercise and always gets improved results. It's also possible to do this exercise alone. I've seen this one exercise move work forward by leaps and bounds.

Very early in my career, I was in a play with the late

Edward (Eddie) Arnold, a character actor I'd seen in many films. The play took place on a farm. In rehearsals, the more confident he became, the more "hammy" I thought he became. I was nervous on opening night. My first line to him was, "How much you want to get for them hogs, Sam? The "H" and "S" wound up getting reversed, and the line came out "How much you want to get for them Sogs, Ham!" He shot me a dirty look. In the next part of the scene, the phone rings and Sam answers it. A neighbor wants to borrow a piece of machinery and Sam says, "Sure, you can pick it up." They converse, and he hangs up. I had a short break during this section of the scene, and turned to my "actress wife" and, under my breath, said, "Oh damn, I can't believe I called him a ham." Well, this night, instead of his phone conversation, I thought I heard Eddie Arnold say, "It's for you, Foss" – my character's name. Like a drowning man, all the rehearsals went through my mind in a flash, and that line was not in any of them. I turned toward Sam, and sure enough, he was holding the receiver straight out toward me. I panicked, gave him a pleading look, and with a broad smile he repeated, "It's for you, Foss," and waved the receiver toward me. All my acting classes flashed before me. Relaxation, I thought. It saved my life! I staggered to the phone, and was able to relax enough to gather my wits and say, "No, I don't have one – but Sam does." I picked up Arnold's hand, clapped the receiver firmly in it, and hurried back to my seat. From then on, whenever I got in trouble on stage, I automatically thought, RELAXATION. It saved me many times and I pass the tip on to you. You may never need it, but if you do – it's magic!

Sometime after relating this incident to my students, I was sitting in the Actors Studio when a voice close behind me whispered, "It's for you, Foss." I stiffened, then relaxed. I turned to find the grinning face of Bruce Dern, a former student. He's quite a tease and loved the instant reaction he got from me every other time he tried it.

Relaxation is a tool that affects all the other tools, as well as all of acting, and all our lives.

ACTUALIZING THE SELF

SENSORY RELIVING

In life, the senses work normally. It's when the actor goes on stage and tension sets in that his senses don't function normally and he looks phony.

Tool number one (Relaxation) supports tool number two (Sensory Reliving), which in turn supplies the foundation for the next step in a steady growth line that builds to a practical "process" that will allow you to perform with confidence any style of material, in any media, anytime, anywhere.

We get our most direct, immediate knowledge of the real world around us through our senses – what we see, hear, smell, touch, and taste. The more acute our senses, and the more input we can get from them, the more output we can create as actors. Heightened senses make for a heightened person, and a heightened person can make for a heightened actor. We're strongly attracted to an actor onstage whose sense of seeing, hearing, smelling, tasting, and touching is more alive than anyone else's. For instance, when an actor with heightened senses kisses a partner onstage, everyone in the audience will experience that kiss. We get more information for our acting from the world and nature if our senses are more aware and alive.

Sensory exercise is probably the most rewarding overall training tool available to an actor. It touches on just about everything you need. It trains you to make real what is imaginary, the basic mandate of the actor. It also develops highly trained observation, concentration, sensitivity, awareness, a sense of truth, and openness to feeling. It makes the unconscious more accessible, a powerful asset for any artist.

In addition to being an excellent training tool, sensory reliving is used directly as an acting tool on stage. You're offered tea or colored water and must treat it as a strong alcoholic beverage. You see an imaginary carriage approaching offstage, you smell an artificial rose as if real, you touch a cheap object as if it were priceless. If it's real for you, it will be real for the audience. One real moment calls forth another real moment. But one unrealized moment leads to another empty moment. The dominos fall one by one – either for you or on top of you.

The actor is someone who possesses the ability to make an imaginary story real for an audience. He acquires this ability by practice. The following exercises will give you a chance to practice this skill as well as enhance your senses for a richer life.

EXERCISE

Sensory Reliving

Start the practice by using simple everyday objects; washing your hands and face (soap and water), shaving (razor, cream),or putting on makeup (lipstick, liner, etc.), dressing (shoes, socks, etc.), eating (lemon, etc.). and drinking (coffee, etc.). Later the list can be expanded.

Let's choose brushing your teeth. For touch, feel the smoothness of the surface of the tube of paste, feel the sides, the bottom; feel the top, the cap, the temperature. Squeeze the tube. Feel the soft paste moving inside the plastic outer shell, sense how this squeezing changes the shape of the tube. What other tactile sensations do you feel? Now, with your sense of touch, not your mind, memorize the tube of paste, much as a blind person might.

Next, put the real tube of paste aside and create an imaginary one by using your tactile memory of the real toothpaste. Duplicate the exact same movements you used for the real paste, leaving empty space where the real object would be. Feel the imaginary object – not your real fingers. Pick up the imaginary tube and explore it in detail. Don't be discouraged if it doesn't feel real at first. Go back to the real tube to get more sensory information. This time get a sense of its weight. What muscles are called into play to lift it? What muscles in your fingers, your hand, wrist, arms, shoulder? Add weight to your imaginary tube. Go back and forth from the real tube to the imaginary tube until you feel less and less difference between them. Don't try to perfect each step; move on to the next one. It will get easier as each step enhances the one following it.

Next, take the top off the tube, feeling the ridges around the cap and the resistance as you turn it. Then smell the paste. What scent do you encounter? Fresh mint? Does it stimulate your nose, have a pungency, a sweetness? Does it remind you of anything? Put the real paste aside and pick up the imaginary tube, unscrew the cap and recreate the odors of the real tube by sensory recollection. Now concentrate on the taste, which is closely connected to smell. Sense sweetness, bitterness, pungency, saltiness, texture, etc.

Using the sense of sight, see the tube in great detail.

Observe the hue of the colors. Are they bright or dull? Notice the design and shapes, details of lettering, etc. When you feel you know every visual nuance of the object, then reach for your imaginary tube and talk out the various details of what you observed. "There are three colors over-all," for instance. "There's a round red logo to the left with white lettering; next to the logo there's a blue oblong shape with large white letters," etc. Whenever you need more information, go back to the real tube.

To go further with your senses, practice making real an imaginary toothbrush using the same technique you used for the toothpaste. Next apply the real paste to the real brush and experience brushing your teeth with full sensory awareness. Hear the sound; taste, smell, and feel the sensa-tions. Now rinse your mouth and do the same procedure with the imaginary toothpaste and brush.

Most people make real what is already real, whereas the actor can make real what is imaginary. That's what we do as a profession. Practice with simple, familiar objects. Later, when you tackle complicated parts like Hamlet, you'll use exactly the same procedure. Hamlet is imaginary to you and your job as an actor is to make him real for an audi-ence. First you must make him real for yourself. The sens-es and awareness of the senses are the keys. Go to some-thing real to get your information. If you're playing Hamlet and need to experience his grief at the loss of his father, recall a time when you lost something important to you, a beloved person or perhaps a pet. Experience a time when someone close to you disappointed you as Hamlet's mother did him; a time when someone betrayed you, as Hamlet's uncle did him. As you did with the toothpaste, go back and forth from your real experiences to the imaginary experi-ences of Shakespeare's Hamlet. More details on exactly how you do this will be covered in Tool #5. Don't despair. The longer you work, the easier it becomes.

All of the following exercises will use this same procedure. Refer back, if necessary. The exercises are primarily for training you as an instrument for acting. They're not directly for the audience. A boxer may train his timing with a jump rope, though he won't be jumping rope in the ring. The better trained the actor's instrument, the more the audience will benefit.

EXERCISES

For Sensory Reliving

Begin all sensory work by neutralizing the self, relaxing thoroughly. (Tool #1)

Touch

Lie on a carpeted floor or textured surface. With both palms down, let the sensitive nerve endings in your fingertips experience the texture of the carpet. Explore the roughness, the smoothness. Feel the depth and thickness of the nap. Examine the backing to which the nap is fastened. Notice the composition of the material, the temperature. Are there any flaws or seams, pieces of grit or foreign matter, any irregularities? You may ask questions with your mind, but be sure to answer with your senses. When you've received enough tactile sensory information from the carpet, raise your hands about four inches above the carpet, and, moving your fingers, recreate the carpet by sensorially reliving it. Ask the same questions you asked of the real carpet, remembering to answer with your senses, not your head. To get more information, to make the imaginary carpet even more real, always go back to the source, in this case the real carpet. Now go back and forth, always lessening the differ-ence between the real carpet and the imaginary one Be careful not to deceive yourself, nor to expect perfection. The result gets fuller with diligent practice.

Next, relax again and, with eyes closed, go back in time as far as you can, to your childhood. Find a remembered significant touch, perhaps your baby blanket, stuffed animal or other toy, pet, a meaningful person from your life, or any souvenir from your past. Using both hands, imaginatively reach out and let your hands relive the object in great detail through your senses. It's very important in all this work that past memories don't remain in your head but result in present sensations. As you touch the item – or person – in your memory, let feelings, sensations, and thoughts con-nected with it come up. Be visceral. Experience it with your whole being. Let whatever happens happen. If nothing happens, don't worry. The effort alone is helpful and the ability will grow. Use as many of your senses as possible. See the object, smell it, touch it, sound it, taste it. (A detailed review of this will be presented later in the book..)

This seemingly simple exercise introduces us to some of the most important basic principles of acting. Fundamentally, acting is making real the imaginary. When you feel the real carpet, you're not acting, but when you raise your hand four inches above the real carpet and recre-ate it, it's as if you're acting. In life, when we're being real in a real dramatic situation, we're (usually) not acting. On the stage, when we're real in an imaginary situation, we are acting. The exercise also shows you the only place to get the information you need to act something – the source, reality itself. (In this case, the real carpet; in a play, your real experiences.) Always start from reality. The senses awaken imprints of past feelings in the present that can be used to stimulate feelings as needed. Carry this exercise into your daily life by becoming acutely aware of everything you touch. Explore touch until you automatically heighten this sense. In addition to your acting, you're enhancing your experience of life.

Adding a foundation of REALITY and TRUTH to any theatrical work gives it an authenticity that intensifies its theatricality. Work on all sensory reliving exercises in intervals of about twenty minutes, followed by a break, as many times in a day as possible for as many days as you can, until it becomes an ingrained habit to be sensorially alive.

EXERCISE

Sensory Reliving

Sound

Relax in any comfortable position. Tune in to the sounds of your own body. Your body is a cacophony of sounds at all times: heart beating, blood coursing, lungs bellowing, food digesting with gurgles and bubbles and so on. Now, listen to the sounds immediately outside your body. Next, listen to the sounds inside the room as a whole. Then listen to the sounds outside your room. Keep stretching until you're listening to the farthest sound you can hear.

This exercise of simply listening for sounds is similar to acting at your best; that is, you won't act listening, you'll listen. You won't pretend to be listening, and won't, for now, play a character listening. Each character listens according to the situation. If you can grasp this principle, you have embraced a core lesson of acting.

Listen intently to a repeatable sound, like music on a disk or tape, for a while. Then stop the sound and "listen" with your memorized senses to the same sound. Go back and forth between the actual sound and the relived sound until you can "hear" it when it's not playing. You're sensitizing your listening for the stage.

Next, find a significant sound from your distant past and relive it, as you did with your sense of touch, letting in feelings, sensations, thoughts, and so on.

In addition to touch, add a heightened awareness of sound to your daily activities until it becomes an unconscious habit. The more you take in, the more you have to give out as an actor.

EXERCISE

Sensory Reliving

Smell Awareness

Relax. Be aware of the smell of your own body. Each body has a unique smell; a bloodhound could pick out your smell even after many people and animals had crossed your path. From your own body, you may smell cosmetics, perfume, shaving lotion, detergent, shampoo, perspiration, and many other scents. Extend your awareness until it includes the whole room. Are odors coming from outside the room? Different seasons bring different smells. Once again, carry this awareness into your daily life.

Relax again and find a meaningful smell from your past – a particular holiday smell, a person, place, or thing; the more details, the better. Work with smell the same way you did with the other senses. Take a specific odor like perfume or limburger cheese and memorize the smell (without it touching the skin directly). Put the real object aside, wash your hands, and relive the odor with your rehearsed sense of smell. Relive it with sensitivity in the now. Smell is the oldest and often the most significant of all the senses. Smell goes directly into the limbic system of the brain, the center of emotions, sexuality, and drive. Nothing can evoke a time, a place, or a past emotion better than an aroma. (Just ask Marcel Proust.) The actor would do well to develop this important sense for himself.

EXERCISE

Sensory Reliving

Taste

Neutralize any tension. Start with the taste in your own mouth. Do you detect any lingering remnants of what you last ate or drank: toothpaste, cigarettes, chewing gum? Do you detect anything sweet, salty, sour, bitter? Become acutely aware of tastes in your everyday life.

Relax, find a taste from your past and relive it in detail. Taste and smell are closely connected. Try eating food while holding your nose. It's difficult to tell an apple from a potato.

Take a lemon wedge and taste and smell it. Put the real lemon aside. Wash your hands thoroughly to remove the real smell. Now, using your senses, pick up the imaginary piece of lemon and taste and smell it. Go from the real lemon to the imagined one with a break and a hand wash between them as they get closer and closer to being the same.

We use the same procedure in rehearsal of a play. In essence, we add real experiences of our own to the imagined events given to us by the playwright until they're virtually the same.

In performance you may have to taste whiskey when drinking colored water. If done fully with the senses, the audience will imaginatively taste the spirits with you. It will enhance their visceral experience of the play.

EXERCISE

Sensory Reliving

Seeing

Close your eyes and relax. Relax the muscles around your eyes, your eyebrows, eyelashes, eyelids. Rest your eyeballs on the bottom of your eye sockets by letting your eyelids feel heavy. Let your eyes drift open softly, and when you're ready, open your eyes gently. Slowly look around the space you're in with soft eyes, as if seeing it for the first time, like a baby. Look at it in the manner of an artist or painter who is planning to draw it from memory. In your daily life, train yourself to look at everything as if you plan to paint it on a canvas, in detail, from memory. Notice something new about familiar things. Colors may get brighter and every-thing will look sharper.

Find objects or works of art that are visually stimulating, observe in great detail the real, and then, removing the object, relive it with your imprinted senses.

Now, relive significant sights from as far back in your life as possible by recalling a meaningful visual stimulus such as a toy, pet, crib, person, blanket, or room. It helps to talk it through. As you do so, let images, feelings, sensations and other sensory stimuli come up. This exercise helps the actor develop a more expressive countenance and often reveals his inner thoughts to the audience. If your eyes are highly sensitized and your facial muscles relaxed, it's as if we can see your thoughts. On film, especially in close-ups, the eyes are truly the mirrors of the soul.

EXERCISE

Sensing a Meaningful Object

Take a "personal object" that has emotional meaning, such as an object given to you by someone no longer living or a significant personal letter from someone special. In Act One, Scene five of *Macbeth*, Lady Macbeth enters reading a moving letter from her husband. The actress could use the personal object exercise at home with a real, emotionally meaningful letter (or other significant object) to give reality to the scene.

She'd work with her real letter by first seeing it in great detail: the envelope, the stamp, the seal, the writing, the signature, the folds; the smell of the letter, if any; the sound of paper as it crinkles and unfolds; the feel of the envelope and paper, the weight. She'd then read the letter and personalize the writer. Her fantasies could then take over and she could let whatever feelings, sensations, and emotions that may come up rise to the surface. She'd then transfer these real feelings to the letter she's to read as Lady Macbeth. The audience will sense the authentic feelings. They'll believe they're coming from the stage letter ("dictated" by Shakespeare), but in fact the actress will be reliving her own, emotionally significant letter.

Any object that has sentimental value can be used in such a circumstance. Later, you can even put this object into your acting space or on your costume to promote a particular feeling. For now, see, touch, and listen to the object, smell and taste it. Do this until the feelings or emotions associated with it are allowed to surface in the present. Later, you can associate these feelings to the words of a play.

It's through the five senses that the outer world becomes

real for us. If a personal object is made real for us through the senses, then that real feeling will surface as it does when you come across a meaningful object or memento in life. Since what you're thinking on stage is personal and private, you can substitute any thought that will bring up feelings for you. The audience won't be aware of the source. They'll think these feelings are coming from the imaginary events and objects of the play itself. Gradually, the actor's personal feelings *will* fully blend and meld with the play.

Sensory Rehearsing

When actors ask what more they can do between classes, on vacation, or when alone, I suggest they do "sensory awareness with rehearsal." Like relaxation, sensory awareness is primarily a training tool, even though both may be used directly when acting.

As reported in *The New York Times* on July 2, 1996, Dr. Daniel Schacter of Harvard led a research team that discovered – by using a PET scan, a diagnostic tool enabling them to view the brain at work recalling a memory – that a memory uses sensory details to complete its "truth." He also discovered that imagined events can be incorporated into this truth. He confirmed what I, as an acting teacher, have suspected for some time.

EXERCISE

Sensory Rehearsing

Start with simple objects that have strong sensory stimuli such as a lemon wedge for taste, perfume for smell, a favorite recording for sound, a piece of silk or burlap for touch, and, for sight, a significant painting or sculpture. Later on, more subtle and complicated objects may be used.

As you did in the introduction to sensory work, memorize the object with your senses, not your mind. With the information you get from the real object, recreate the imaginary one from the memorized sensory stimulus. The difference is that now you can rehearse on your own in great detail, as you would an actual production. Rehearse until you feel the imaginary object has become nearly as fully "real" as the original. Work with the same object in the same place at the same time each time you rehearse. An action that you perform in life, like drinking a cup of coffee, may take a few moments to get. The same action done with an *imaginary* stimulus (no coffee cup to practice on) may take a few hours because of the in-depth concentration on details needed. Work in 20-minute intervals, at least twice a day if practical, for as many days as possible. The difference between sensory rehearsing and the sensory tooth brushing exercise we did earlier is the rehearsing aspect. You approach sensory rehearsing more as you would the steps for a stage production. You also do it over a longer period of time, and you could present it to a coach, or others if you choose, for feedback. It's more presentational.

When you've worked with a variety of simple objects, expand to more complex combinations of sensory and physical stimulus. Take hot and cold showers or baths, first

real, then imaginary, while at the same time tasting something real, then imaginary, and then combining them at the
same time, under different weather conditions. And so on.
Don't imitate – create. Don't pantomime, using the physical
aspects only. Pantomime is closer to dance than to acting.
If you develop the joy of creation right from the beginning
you can have a long and happy career!

TOOL #3

ACTUALIZING THE SELF

PHYSICAL RELIVING

Acting is too rich to be done only with the conscious mind.

Just as the five senses are intricately bound to our feelings and emotions by the brain's circuitry, so is our kinesthetic sense (or moving body in space), sometimes called the sixth sense. You cannot cry or laugh, get mad or frightened, without physical manifestations of some kind. The body has a kind of "memory" or awareness of its own connected to the brain's circuitry.

The following exercises will develop your "muscle imagination," and result in an expressive body that performs with grace and vitality free of the inhibitions that can hold back your full talent.

The introduction to physical awareness is much the same as for sensory awareness, in practice. Work with the real to get information, and then use this information to make the imaginary real.

To deeply understand and get full benefit from the following exercises, you must DO them with your full physical self. As with all the exercises, appreciating their logic on the page won't help you on the stage. Work in 20-minute intervals twice a day – more if possible.

EXERCISE

Physical Reliving

The Imaginary Body

Begin with a standing relaxation. This may prove useful when you need to relax onstage. For a quick standing relaxation, balance each part of the body one on top of the other, starting from the bottom and working upward. Plant your feet firmly on the floor, then balance each ankle over each foot, each knee over each lower leg, and so on, up to the head. Then balance each part starting from the head and working down. Feel so balanced that there seems to be no effort or energy required to stand.

A deeper way to relax begins with full awareness of each part of the body. While standing, mentally scan the entire body beginning with the feet and working upward in greater detail. Be aware of each toe, the nails, the spaces between toes. What temperature are they? Is each moist or dry? Next, put your attention on the bottom of each foot and its contact with the ground, the crease where toes join the ball of the foot, inside arch and outside rim, heel, top of foot, Achilles tendon, ankle, and so on up the entire body in great detail. This is the same procedure we used earlier while lying on our backs.

From a relaxed and balanced standing position, stretch your right arm slowly over your head with concentrated attention. Be keenly aware of everything that happens in your entire body, from your scalp down to your toes, as you reach high above your head. Lower your arm with the same degree of attention. It will help, especially in the beginning, to quietly verbalize what's happening, such as "I am stretching my arm and I feel the shoulder muscles tighten," etc. Verbalize in order to deepen the awareness. Repeat this movement several times.

Now, with your arms stationary at your sides through- out the exercise, without any actual real movement, raise and lower your imaginary right arm. Talk out the process in detail.

Again stretch your real right arm over your head, absorbing even more information and detail. Then, with arms at your sides, raise your imaginary right arm. Alternate several times between your real and imaginary right arms as the difference between the real and imaginary actions decreases. Repeat the same procedure with the left arm.

Next, raise your real right arm and your imaginary left arm, then your real left arm and imaginary right arm. Try raising both arms at the same time – first both real arms, then both imaginary arms.

Pinwheel your real right arm backward then forward from the shoulder in large circles. Then pinwheel your imaginary right arm the same way. When you're ready, repeat this motion with the left arm. Now do it with the real right arm and the imaginary left arm, then alternate. You can then pinwheel forward with one arm while backward with the other, mixing real and imaginary movements as you wish.

Spin your whole body, first in one direction and then in the opposite direction. Then spin your real body in one direction and imaginary body in the other at the same time. It's also OK to have fun!

You can use any movements or combinations of move- ments your imagination dictates. Try this approach with any movements you may have difficulty with in sports, dance, or any other activity that you want to improve. You will be surprised at the positive results.

EXERCISE

Physical Reliving

Advanced Scene Work

Sometime in the future, when you've learned more acting tools and developed your muscle imagination and awareness, and you've worked on a scene fully, you may want to try doing the scene, or a difficult part of it, with your imaginary body. Don't just think the scene, relive it fully with the imaginary body, both inner and outer. You may take any position you want, but keep your real body still while doing the lines silently. Since it's in your imagination, you can do the scene ideally, to perfection. The ideal body has no limitations, fears, inhibitions, or blocks. Then, repeat the scene vocally with your real body. Alternate the two, also adding the senses (Tool #2).

Strongly resist imitating the imaginary body when you redo the scene with the real body. Trust that something has grown and forget it. At first, the real may not feel as good as the imaginary, but as your skills grow, the real and the "ideal imaginary" will coincide. You can rehearse in this manner almost anywhere, anytime, since it's all in the mind. Working on the imaginary body isn't an end in itself. It's a means to make the body more real in the imaginary world of theatre. But don't attempt this exercise until you've done the rest of the work and have fully rehearsed the real.

Physical reliving is an excellent training tool for developing physical awareness, consciousness, and physical dynamics that evoke feeling and enhance your physical presence.

Many athletes work with the imaginary body. They physically relive the perfect execution of their sport, using their imagination, just before they execute the real movements. A diver will stand on the edge of the board and imaginatively go through a perfect dive just before she dives. Bob Beaton, the sports psychologist, uses these visualization techniques when working with Olympic athletes. He says, "In addition to being 100 percent physically fit, you need to have equal mental fitness and attitude." The author and trainer Jean Houston uses these mind techniques with equally gratifying results.

EXERCISE

Physical Reliving

Physical Reliving With Rehearsal

Find a specific, real physical task, like lifting and carrying a very heavy object, such as a toolbox from one place to another and putting it down with a follow–through (as in sports where, after you hit the ball, you continue to follow through the movement). Always have a definite reason for doing the task – for example, lifting and carrying a heavy suitcase to a van for a summer vacation trip. Be aware of everything happening in your entire body from top to bottom. Now relive the task exactly the same way without the real object. Go back and forth between the real object and the imaginary one. Rehearse about twenty minutes, a few times a day, until you're satisfied there's as little difference as possible between the real physical task and the imaginary one.

You'll notice this is the same procedure we used for the sensory work, going to the real to get information to create the imaginary, only this time we're doing it with the physical body.

You can do this exercise using a variety of objects and physical conditions. Imagine, for example, you're carrying a container filled to the brim with nitroglycerin; if a few drops are spilled, you'll blow up. (Practice this one with water, please!)

Other possible activities include walking on a moving vehicle, such as a bus, subway, boat, or escalator, or walking while extremely tired. Carry this physical awareness into your everyday life. Eventually you'll "own" this physical richness and bring an added dimension to your acting. This last exercise is used with great success by the actress and teacher Uta Hagen in her classes at the H.B. Studio in New York City.

TOOL #4

NEUTRALIZING THE SCRIPT
TO ACTUALIZE IT MORE FULLY

If you want to find the truth of anything, you must first come to neutral, and strip away all you know before it gets in the way of finding anything new.

I observed when I first started teaching that actors were coming to me with ingrained bad acting habits obtained from many previous sources. We wasted a great deal of time trying to erase these inhibiting habits. A technique called neutralizing was found to solve this problem. We've already discussed neutralizing the self (Tool #1). Now we will neutralize the script.

Suppose I discover a cure for all physical and mental illness. I go to a blackboard to record my formula and find it covered with numbers and letters. I'd better erase that blackboard before starting my work, or my formula will be lost in the jumble of old thinking. Even novice actors, with their heads filled with TV, film, and stage performances, have accumulated a jumble of notions about what acting "should be." Even if they've already worked with some teachers or directors, they may have picked up some bad habits that are now imprinted on their subconscious.

A well-tuned piano is neutral; it doesn't care if I play contemporary or classical music on it. A true artist would not want to sit down to play an antique "player piano" with a fixed mechanical roll playing on it. Yet many actors do exactly that. So, first you "clean house" by neutralizing the script; then you can actualize the script.

When I work with actors for the first time, I like to start them out in "neutral." Even actors who've acted a variety of characters in different styles may need to start a new role in neutral. Like relaxation, neutralization is a temporary means, not an end. Learning to neutralize a script is not just for beginning actors; it can often be even more beneficial to established actors who want to start fresh, or try a new approach.

In Tool #1 we dealt with neutralizing the actor through relaxation, stripping him down to pure innocence with the potential to go anywhere. Now with this tool we want to bring the script unencumbered to an original core where the actor, director, and playwright can take it anywhere their talent dictates.

Neutral in itself is not necessarily "good." You won't be asked to achieve it in performance. Your first objective is to eradicate any false tendencies. If you can remove only 50 percent of the "bad," then you can, at best, put in only 50 percent "good." Until it becomes a habit, you learn to neutralize everything so you can add what you choose. Neutral is a blank canvas; you don't want to start with a picture already on the easel. Neutral is like the "Beginner's Mind" of Zen. The mind of the beginner is empty, free of the habits of the expert, ready to accept, to doubt, and open to all possibilities. As a neutral actor, you're not directly trying to make something great, but simply acting with full openness, as if you're discovering what you're doing for the first time. You do this moment-to-moment each time you act. You're not, then, merely repeating the patterns that feel safe, patterns you've copied, consciously or unconsciously, from other actors. Instead, you work from what arises spontaneously from the real moment.

Here are some suggestions for approaching a part in neutral. These guidelines are important for beginning the work; they become less so as you internalize them in the Process.

EXERCISE

Neutralizing the Script

For good neutral work, after you select your material, or have been cast, don't study directly from the book or script. It's best to have someone else copy it for you (otherwise, do it yourself) without any instructions given by the playwright on what to do. The copy should be dialogue only, with no stage directions or parenthetical comments. Copy it with no capital letters and absolutely no punctuation of any kind. No periods, commas, dashes – just words. You got the general meaning from the initial reading. Only bad actors – and some uptight characters – speak with studied or stressed punctuation. Learn the lines, neutrally and relaxed, from this specially prepared copy. It may be difficult for you to speak without punctuation; however, do the best you can. It's an exercise to free you from phony formality. Punctuation came along with writing. People communicated long before punctuation.

Remember, neutrality is a temporary means to an end, not an end in itself. Its purpose is to erase or prevent the unconscious intrusion of "bad" acting habits and clichés such as reading the lines the way every other actor does who follows the punctuation slavishly. Sometimes the script can sound stilted and formal. Acting is not after all about the words per se, but what lurks behind them and motivates them.

Neutral means:

◆ NO punctuation of sentences as you memorize the dialogue.

◆ Breathe in the middle of a thought – not at the breaks.

◆ NO feelings or emotions.

◆ NO interpretation, emphasis, or underlining words.

◆ NO figuring out "how to do it."

◆ NO meaning, analysis, concepts, judgments.

◆ NO form, style.

◆ NO pacing.

◆ NO phrasing, patterns, music, or rhythm to the lines (don't "sing" them).

◆ NO being tense, fixed, or set – you need to be able to drop the neutral later.

It's difficult to describe exactly how to do neutral without negating the benefits. As soon as you follow someone else's description, you're not neutral anymore! "Rote" and "mechanical" are not neutral; they're "rote" and "mechanical." There's no exact name or label you can put on it. It's the actor's equivalent of the stillness that accentuates the movements of a dancer, the silence that highlights the sound of an orchestra or singer.

For positive, productive neutral:

◆ Don't put your words on tape, audio or video.

◆ Don't work in front of a mirror.

(The reason for these two is that you may memorize and imitate your early recorded "bad" habits and patterns. You need to allow for growth as your work gets richer.)

◆ Don't pace as you work; it robs you of spontaneous movements and the two activities become associated.

TOOL #5

ACTUALIZING THE SCRIPT

EMOTIONAL RELIVING EXPERIENCING

You cannot truly act what you have not experienced in essence.

Up until now we have been tuning the actor as an "instrument"; now we start to "play that instrument."

As with the previous tools, the experience tool is both a training tool and is also used directly in your acting. It is a training tool when it opens your emotions. It is an acting tool when your character needs to express true emotions that are not readily accessible to you.

"Experiencing" is one of the most important, controversial, and difficult of all the tools; it can also be the most rewarding. You will need patience and concentration. Even if you do not use this tool directly in your acting, it is an excellent training tool. It will sensitize your feelings and emotional life and give your acting greater depth. It is actually difficult to be phony when you are coming from reality.

The danger in learning lines early on is that they become set. Learned in neutral, the lines are flexible and can go in any direction you or the director want. I think of the lines per se as a technical component for the actor. The words represent the artistry of the playwright. For the actors, it's what they do with the lines, how they humanize them through their own full being, that makes them artistic collaborators with the playwright.

The purpose of the following steps is to lead you to the important underlying experience the actor is feeling between, around, and under the words the character speaks. The steps themselves are not the destination; they are the guideposts.

Emotional Reliving

Ask yourself, after learning the lines well in neutral (Tool #4): "In order for this character to use these particular words at this specific time, which of the following four emotional states best reflects her experience at the deepest level – underneath the words – SAD, MAD, GLAD, or FEARFUL?" Of course, there are many kinds and degrees of each of these feelings. For our present purpose, we can be very general and loose, getting more specific and refined as we go on. Just about all real experiences will have elements of at least three of these four feelings in different degrees. Like a good diamond, the more facets your experience reflects, the more brilliantly it will shine. If you look deeply, a feeling is never single-faceted. In painting, the primary colors of red, blue, and yellow can be mixed to form most other colors. In the same way, for the actor, sadness, anger, gladness, and fear can be mixed to form many other feelings.

Now name the four emotions in order of their dominance for the character. For example, "At this point, I feel the character that is saying these words is, at the deepest level, experiencing primarily sadness, then fear, then anger."

The next step is to figure out the overall dramatic event that is facing the character. To help find this event, finish the sentence, "It's like when. . . ." For instance, at this time I think what the character is experiencing is like when someone you love betrays or abandons you. The main purpose of the "like when" step is to force you to confront the circumstances facing the character that can then lead you to more accurately find the important next steps.

After you rough out the feelings of the character, you are ready to make the material more specifically personal to you. To do this, ask, "when in my life have I experienced, IN ESSENCE, this same kind of experience?" The words "in essence" are very important! By essence I mean you don't have to literally have had the same experience as your character, but a similar experience that at the core is essentially the same. As an example, an actress named Becky was playing the part of Lady Torrance in Tennessee Williams' *Orpheus Descending*, in which the character's greatest desire is realized when she discovers she is pregnant. The actress was concerned about how to approach the part since she was never pregnant. Asked about the happiest moments of her own life, Becky relived a time when her family moved to Israel. Her father strongly suggested she do something to help her country. Becky joined the army and was assigned to the Air Force. She was horrified to find she was expected to parachute at a great height from an airplane. She immediately went to her instructor and said it would be impossible. He assured her that she would be well trained beforehand and not to be concerned. The day came when she found herself going up for her first jump. She was in denial and numb when it was her turn to go out the door and into space. She became panic–stricken. She said, "No, I can't do it!" Her instructor said, "Nonsense. You are well trained and a good student. Just remember everything and jump!" He gently but firmly helped her out the door. Adrenalin shot through her and everything she learned came back in a flash, as her instructor knew it would. The next thing Becky knew, she was sailing through the air exalted. She landed, pulled her chute in, and sat on the ground joyously thinking about how proud her father would be. The actress glowed with fulfillment and pride as she transferred these feelings to the words of the play. Everyone watching was deeply moved. Since she never experienced the pregnancy the character had, Becky picked an experience of her own that she felt had essentially the same essence as the character's. It worked beautifully and the audience never suspected she had just completed a parachute jump. The audience will understand what the words of the play suggest. In essence the triumph was the same for the joy of the jump and the joy of the pregnancy. While it may take some probing, I have yet to find anyone who has not been able to find an experience parallel in its essence. Becky now knew she could have the character's full experience. The next step was to associate the feelings to the playwright's words.

Another example from a play would be: You are playing Hamlet; you soon discover he is confused and can't make up his mind what action to take. Find a time in your life when you had an important and difficult decision to make, and you agonized over what direction to take. Relive this experience (as outlined below) and transfer your feelings and emotions to this aspect of Hamlet.

The steps, so far, to using the tool of experience are:

1. Learning the lines in neutral.
2. Asking what the character is experiencing at this

time, using the formula of sad, mad, glad, afraid.

3. Putting the feelings in order of their dominance.

4. Answering the "it's like when . . ." question.

5. Asking, "When in my life have I experienced, in essence, this same kind of experience, going as far back in my life as is possible?" (The further back you go, the more reliable the experience is because it's settled in.) For instance, if you were to use anger from the break–up of a current romance, that anger and the experience could be lost if he sends you a dozen roses the next day with a sincere note telling you how sorry he is and how much he loves you.

All the previous tools you have worked on will be called into use – the neutral work, the relaxation, the sensory and physical reliving. Each and every tool is a vital link to the whole process of acting and each must be worked on thoroughly before moving on to the next. While answering the above questions, you are also discovering your character on the deepest level.

The sixth and final step to forging the experience tool is to actually experience your parallel event in the present and then to integrate it with the playwright's words, which you have learned neutrally. It's a way of acting that works the way nature itself functions.

As reported in *The New York Times*, October 25, 1994, research scientists like Dr. Larry Cahill and associates are excited about something they have just discovered but which some acting teachers have understood for years: the brain has two memory systems, one for ordinary information and one for emotionally charged information. The actor consciously takes advantage of and strengthens our system for strong emotional memory. Haven't you many times thought of some past traumatic event and suddenly felt yourself experiencing real feelings of anger, sadness, or joy? Our consciousness shifts at such times from where we are now to another time and place and genuine feelings come up. We all have the ability to fully relive past events in the present. In everyday life, this happens haphazardly. In the art of acting, we take advantage of this ordinary, natural ability and make it a specific tool. We intentionally call up feelings on cue. As we practice this skill, it gets easier and richer. Many actors, sadly, just imitate life. It is always an imitation of the real thing, or worse, an imitation of an imitation. At best, acting is the ability to make the imaginary real! Acting is not making something that is already imaginary – imaginary, as so many actors do.

The technique for opening up and capturing these valuable past events for present work is to, in the beginning work, concentrate more on "there" (the original experience) than "here" (the rehearsal room or stage). The actor associates or transfers these feelings to the present work until she no longer has to concentrate on the original event – it is all happening now, in the current work, by association. We will walk through this procedure step–by–step.

Apply the experience tool generally at first. You may want to begin by setting it in time – "I am ten years old." Don't go to the event yet; get the concentration working by capturing the time and space of the event. Who and what else occupy your time, interests, and energy in this past time? Always use the present tense of the past event. Don't say, "I WAS," as if remembering; say, "I AM," reliving it right now. If you ask questions with your mind, answer with your whole being. Are you in school? What grade? Who are your teachers, principal, contemporaries? See each one now! Who is your favorite? Whom don't you like? Do you have a sweetheart or a best friend? See the school building inside and out. Take your time and experience everything fully and in great detail.

Start to get more and more specific now. When you start to get more "there" (past experience) than "here" (present), you may want to focus in closer to the event you chose. Is it a weekday or weekend? What time of year? What time of day? What is the weather like? Where does it happen? See the place very specifically, using all your five senses and physical reliving at all times. What sounds do you hear from outside and in? What smells, touches do you sense? Is there any taste or dryness? What do you see? How are you dressed? How do you feel physically, mentally, spiritually, psychologically? Who else is there? See them specifically.

Experience what happened "there" in great detail. Relive not only what you may have said, but also what wasn't said, what you wanted to say but couldn't manage for some reason. What do you "wish" you had said or done? Often, this is more real than the act you put on at that time. Concentrate more and more on the event to the exclusion of everything else.

When you are "there," and the original feelings come up, transfer the emotions to the playwright's words that you learned in neutral – this is how the words become actualized. Don't push or force or act what "should" be happening to you. Anticipation and expectation are two of the worst killers of real feelings. If nothing happens, don't panic. All is not lost. Relax and stay with it for a while; go over the steps again in greater detail. Try another experience, maybe at another time.

The actress Kim Stanley, while playing in *The Three Sisters*, by Chekhov, found that the emotion that worked so well in a scene suddenly stopped working. She anxiously consulted Lee Strasberg who told her to relax and not go for the result she expected. In the next performance she did not push or have expectations, and the emotion came back and stayed.

Throughout your whole career you may discover only six or seven memories that you can use over and over with shaded changes to fit the specific play or character you are working on. There are only so many basic emotions we humans have with infinite variations.

How will you know when you are "there"? When you experience it viscerally now, when you perspire, or your breathing changes, or you feel hot or cold, your pulse quickens, your face gets red, or other real, physical, mental, psychological sensations occur in the now. (You'll know!)

Again, the experience tool is only valid after it is connected to the current work. There is nothing worse than seeing a glassy-eyed actor preoccupied with a past experience that does not relate to the present play or to the other actors. We use the past only to enrich the present. The bulk of this personal association work is done away from rehearsals and then tried in rehearsals. It should never be done directly in performance for the first time without testing it.

EXERCISE

For Emotional Reliving

Life History

It would be very good at this point to start writing a "life history," an emotional history of your life. Start with your oldest memories. As you write it, let yourself experience all you remember that made an impression on you, or was "dramatic" for you at a pre-school age. Then, as a reference only, go to the first grade, write and relive all the feeling events that involved you emotionally, then go grade by grade through elementary school, high school, etc. When you come to events that evoke strong feelings, you would be wise to transcribe them onto three-by-five cards for fast future reference. You may index them under the headings of sad, mad, glad, and afraid.

The act of recalling, writing out, and reliving these emotional events will start to open up your feelings, sensitize you, and make you more vulnerable, all excellent qualities for an actor. Practically, you will have a present and future reference for emotional recall and transfer to the many parts you will play. You will start to develop Emotional Intelligence (see the book with this title by Daniel Goleman [Bantam Books]).

Dreams can also be used as experiences. Often, we experience stronger feelings and emotions in dreams than we do in life. Dreams can be entered in a separate section of your "life history," mentioned earlier.

Suppose you are playing the character of Biff in *Death of a Salesman* by Arthur Miller, the scene where he discovers his father in a hotel room with a strange woman. You may choose a past experience when you were deeply hurt by the betrayal of a close friend. You then relive that past experience in the present (as outlined earlier) and when the original feelings come up, you would say the lines of Biff and the emotion is transferred to the present play.

In the Process, it's as if in the early rehearsals we don't act the words of the play. We use the words to express the experiences under them, as we do in life. Lesser actors act the words per se. Greater actors don't act the experiences; they have them. The words are conditioned by the experience. It's almost as if you don't act the script in the beginning – you have the experiences. Later they blend in harmony with the interpretation. This is also the best way you can serve the playwright. More about this and about analyzing and interpreting the script later.

NOTE: **Psychology and Acting**

The Process is invariably therapeutic but is never therapy. Everything involving relationships between people involves psychology on some level, so there are bound to be parallels. However, the many differences between acting and therapy are more important. For instance, the therapist is trying to get you to be real, to tell the full truth to yourself, in real life situations, while the actor's goal is to be real in imaginary situations. The ultimate aim of therapy is opposite to that of acting. Essentially, the therapist wants you to function more productively in everyday life, while the actor's aim is to function more productively in an art form.

I promise my therapist friends that I will not practice therapy when I teach acting if they will not teach acting when they do therapy.

TOOL #6

NEUTRALIZING AND ACTUALIZING YOUR ACTING PARTNERS

PERSONALIZING

The selfish actor thinks he alone is the actor.

As actors we try to make everything as theatrically real and personal to us as it is to the character.

You neutralize your acting partners in order to actualize them more fully. Personalizing means to make personal and not general. Actualizing is making real through action.

A true monologue is the kind where Hamlet is alone on stage speaking his private thoughts. A contemporary monologue is usually a dialogue in which only one person speaks. If a dialogue is used as a monologue, it is suggested you have a "listening–responding" actor on stage for you to interact with. You have to imagine this person often in auditions where you may get a robotic stage manager. Then personalizing can be a great help.

You will work with a great diversity of actors, each with his own unique personality. You will have different feelings towards each one, some you like and become friends with, others you will try to avoid. Yet within the play itself, our own personal inclinations must be neutralized before a vibrant stage relationship can develop. After all, a script may call for us to hate someone we genuinely like, or to love someone we hate.

In theater we are often introduced to someone we never met before who will soon become someone we are intimately involved with on stage or screen. In early rehearsals you could personalize them. To do this, it is best if you neutralize them first.

EXERCISES

NEUTRALIZING YOUR ACTING PARTNERS

To "neutralize" your fellow actors, you may try to see them as empty screens or blank canvases. See each one as an ageless, sexless, faceless blank without personality. With your imagination, temporarily blur their image with your eyes if necessary. Erase all the qualities that make them who they are to you personally. It may be difficult but try to find your own way of doing this.

Ultimately, the best way to neutralize your partner is to actualize them as someone with the essence of the qualities you envision them to have that will work for your character. Put your concentration on your personalization or parallel person.

To actualize your partner, first ask how does MY character experience THE OTHER character? Give this some serious thought because you are already analyzing your relationship with your partner. The next important question is: Whom in my present or past life do I experience, "in essence," the same way? If you have to love a character and you are turned off by the actor playing that character, then imaginatively substitute a person you love for that character. (Some people already do this in life.)

Now, let your neutralized acting partner represent that specific parallel person for you. Don't try to put another person's head on your partner. Just let your partner stand in for the parallel person you picked. Let him be a proxy or a double. Slowly, blend your co-actor and the real life parallel person until they are the same for you. Ultimately, you will learn to neutralize them by actualizing them and by concentrating on their being who you want them to be for you, to the exclusion of who they really are. This is accomplished in one step.

Now you have authentic feelings toward your fellow actors and the audience will sense and appreciate it. For example, if the script calls for your character to feel hate and fury with another character, as Mr. Roberts feels toward the Captain in *Mr. Roberts,* you may substitute someone from your own life who you felt was unjust and hurtful to you. Use the same procedure for a role which requires you to have loving feelings toward another character. Allow the feelings to be real instead of imaginary. The play is already imaginary, so bring as much reality to it as possible.

Remember, anything we use from the past must be transferred to the present. The tool is complete only when the feelings of the real past parallel person are blended and become one with the present actor. First you neutralize; then you actualize.

Personalization Exercise

Two partners face each other, standing five or six feet apart. Each pick a parallel figure you hate from any part of your life. Next, personalize your partner as that person. Express your most vitriolic bitterness and feelings toward the parallel person represented by your partner. Both do this vocally, full force, at the same time, without listening or answering your partner. Now, try it with love. (I'm invariably surprised that most find love more difficult than hate.) You may also use this exercise with two lines of actors facing each other.

Intimacy Exercises

Before working with a partner (especially for the first time), try holding each other's hands and, while looking into each other's eyes for a time, let whatever feelings and emotions you feel come up until you're relatively comfortable with each other. All kinds of sensations may surface for each individually, and between the two of you.

If body contact is called for, you may want to explore each other physically in appropriate ways. You may want to hold and hug. This can help get the nervousness out of the way – unless you want that in the scene.

Stand back to back with your partner, close your eyes and make physical contact. Non–verbally say hello and have a conversation with your backs by physically moving. Don't make it a silly game to avoid real feelings. Add hands, arms, legs, head, etc. Let the movements flow into a back–

to–back dance. When ready, non–verbally say good–bye and slowly move apart a short distance. Stay still for a while and experience the separation. In the movie *Junior*, Emma Thompson co–starred with Arnold Schwartzeneggar. When they first met in person, she asked him to lie on the floor. After he obliged, she jumped on him and they rolled playfully all over the floor. Then she got up and said, "Now I can work with you."

Weapons

In a scene where there is aggression or seduction, either passive or overt, choose an imaginary weapon that suits your character and use it imaginatively against or to attract your partner. An imaginary blowgun with darts might be right for a Noël Coward play, with the usual short, sharp barbed words from many of the characters. The blowgun may also work in a number of Shakespeare's plays. Words may become clubs in plays like *The Lion in Winter* by James Goldman. For seduction, you might imagine using a soft, feathered fan or flower. The flower can even have thorns if your imagination dictates, as, for example, in *Dangerous Liaisons*. Have fun choosing the appropriate weapon. Imagine that your words are the weapons to use where and when needed. If you have to say "Are you my bitterest enemy?" as Vanya says in *Uncle Vanya* by Chekhov, you could make each word or the whole sentence a sword to jab at the professor.

You may also use this exercise with two lines of actors facing each other. They practice using different words as weapons or in positive ways between each other.

THE THREE "R'S" OF ACTING

RECEIVE-REACT-RESPOND

Acting is being fully concentrated in the here and now of each moment on the stage.

You receive what your partner is communicating, you react to it, and then you respond with your dialogue. When I say something that's extremely important to me, I worry about how it will be received by others. For example, when I ask a hard- nosed, grouchy boss for a raise which I desperately need, I will watch with great attention for every possible clue as to how he is reacting to my request. Is he angry and about to fire me, or is he receptive and considering it? What is his body language saying? As a result of my observations, I will try to adjust my thinking and strategy. At the same time, the boss is probably aware of my body language. Do I seem strong and resolved, or weak and frightened? As a result of his calculations, his attitude will change. This goes back and forth in a continuous cycle. It happens in a millisecond. We learn it as a baby, and the skill improves. Because a play is repeated many times, we can, unfortunately, forget this real–life behavior.

This listening–reacting circle keeps your concentration flowing. Strong listening skills and the three "R's" of acting – Receiving–Reacting–Responding – can help make you a spe-

cial actor. It may seem elementary, but listening, and especially hearing, is a vital, active part of good acting. We can
get so interested in our own lines that this vital aspect of our
reality is often neglected. Taking in and digesting your partners' lines can make your lines more connected and true to
the moment.

If you ever start to hear your own lines, you are not acting at your best. Immediately shift your consciousness to
your partner. Notice something specific about him or her, or
try to find something you never noticed before. Your best
acting most often comes from a strong sense of connection
with your partner(s).

EXERCISES

For the Three "R's" Juxtapose Real & Imaginary

Start a real conversation with your partner using any subject. Then go back and forth between the playwright's
words as written and your own real dialogue with your
partners. The juxtaposition of the real and the imaginary
will let you know if or when you are being phony when
using the playwright's words alone. This can be a light conversation or it may be a heavy conversation from your own
real, personal life experience – whatever best fits the scene.
You may speak to your real acting partner directly or to your
partner as a parallel personal substitution (Tool #6). For
example, (speaking my real life experience to my partner): "I
know my father loved me, but at times I felt he was too busy
to even notice me, and it hurt." (The playwright's lines as
written): ". . . my wife and I rarely talk to each other anymore. We share the same bed but as two strangers." When

I speak the playwright's lines I am experiencing my real feelings about my father to lend it authenticity. In rehearsal, I start the lines about my father and, with no break, shift to the playwright's lines. There should be little or no difference between them since I am trying to give the playwright's lines reality no matter what the style or period of the play. I can speak my real-life lines semi-audibly or silently in early rehearsals. In production they should be associated as one.

Give and Take

Silently look for something that you can take physically or mentally from your partner before you can give him your line. He does the same with you. You go back and forth, taking and giving, giving and taking. What you take may be something your partner is wearing, a facial expression, something you fantasize, something personal or impersonal, and so on. If I have to feel positive toward you, I might take your open smile or the way you pout or the way I imagine you look in bed. If my character feels negative toward you I may think silently of the messy way you leave your dressing room or your perceived bad acting in a specific scene.

You may learn something about listening by observing how it happens in life. The intensity of our listening varies from moment to moment. If someone is giving us directions or information that can save our lives – how to escape an enemy – we listen attentively. If it's something we know and have heard a thousand times, we listen in a distracted or bored way. Start to observe how, when, and why we listen the way we do. As well as observing yourself listening in life, notice how different people listen differently. We can communicate a great deal about our characters by the way they attend to one another. Notice how individuals make or avoid eye contact. Unless we have a reason, we usually don't make constant, direct eye contact while listening or speaking. Don't act listening, listen! Don't act looking, look!

Actors speak and listen to the same lines over and over, in rehearsal and performance, yet we have to hear them freshly each time, as if for the first time. We really have to work from moment to moment, without anticipating or having expectations. Don't go over your next line while your partners are speaking theirs. Acting between the lines includes listening.

We started by bringing the actor alive as a real–life instrument. First we neutralized, wiping the slate clean by using relaxation (Tool #1); then actualized, by awakening our being using sensory stimulants (Tool #2). Then we worked to make the outer side more alive and involved by working with the body (Tool #3). Next, we worked with the script to activate it (Tools #4 and #5). Finally, we dealt with making other characters real for ourselves (Tools #6 and #7). In the next part, we begin to give action and direction to what we have worked on so far.

TOOL #8

THE BIG THREE

NEEDS-OBSTACLES-STRATEGY

Everything is neutral until we give it intention.

This is the Swiss Army Knife of acting. It has three closely
linked parts which fold into each other: "The Big Three" –

◆ What do I want;
◆ What's in the way of my getting it;
◆ What do I have to do to overcome what's in my way?

PART 1. NEEDS AND INTENTIONS

Most plays get started when a character wants something,
and end when they either get it or fail to get it. The section
in between is about what they do to overcome the obstacles
in the way of getting it. To give your work movement, ask,
"What does my character really need – bottom line?" You
can start with your first impulses, but through rehearsals,
and even performances, keep looking for deeper needs. The
needs may be subconscious for the character, but whatever

is subconscious for the character must always be conscious for the actor playing him. If I take action, whether conscious or unconscious, the result is the same.

Needs can be conceptualized on all levels: biological, psychological, spiritual, mental, social, philosophical. There is no moment in our lives when we are not in need or want or desire of some kind (you are reading this book right now because of one of the above). Even when we sleep, we need to rest for physical health and to dream for mental health. So too, a character is in constant need. There is the need that propels the whole play and the many needs in between, usually connected to the larger need.

Find the deep need, and you find the key to the work. A script should be broken down into "sections of needs." From here to there, I need so and so, and from there to there, I need this, and so on. This is often called breaking the script into "beats." A need works best if expressed as an active verb in its infinitive form (a verb that has "to" before it, such as to seduce, to threaten, and so on). Needs always have consequences, and affect your character's whole life.

You often get what you strongly intend. What do I passionately desire? What is my motive? What am I fighting for? What would winning this need be like, success feel like, victory be like? What ideal result do I envision? The more powerful the character's need, the more powerful the acting.

Needs must always go outward and involve the other actors. In the early days of the Method, the actors were often criticized for not being heard, for contemplating their navel, and so forth. I think this was so because the big three were not emphasized. The very good inner work was not always externalized. This one tool could have helped clear this up.

EXERCISE

The Big Three

Part 1. Needs

Two partners or two lines face each other. One line or one person (A) has some object in his or her open hand (keys, comb, lipstick, etc.). The line or person opposite (B) believes that this object represents his own personal, greatest desire. Working with the partner in line (A), the person in line (B)'s need or intention is to get the person in line (A) to give the object to them using verbal means. The person with the object presents an obstacle by refusing unless she truly believes the (B) person really needs the object, life–or–death. (A) shouldn't be too easy to persuade – or impossibly resistant either. If (B) can't achieve the objective with kindness, he or she should use threats or any other verbal means – never physical. Like most exercises, all parties should remain themselves, and should not do it as a character, unless doing it for a specific play and character.

Part 2. Obstacles

The second part of the "Big Three" is the obstacle to getting your needs met. The actor who can understand and master the obstacle tool will always be an exciting and highly dramatic player. Obstacles are the essential ingredient that make drama exciting. We may dream of a life with no obstacles, but once animated people have cleared all their obstacles away, they promptly create new ones to keep life stimulating.

All sports depend on obstacles to stimulate excitement. A football game, for instance, depends heavily on the "Big Three" to hold our interest. Someone introducing football to a group that had never seen a game might say, "Well, the goal of this game is the NEED to get the ball between the distant posts" (the goal line). But if that's all there were to it, one team would just pick up the ball and amble down the field and put the ball between the posts. Then, the other team would do the same. Soon, everyone would get bored and leave. We say, "No. Each team has to present an OBSTACLE by needing to keep the other from getting a goal." So, then one team keeps running the ball down the center against the other. It is now more interesting, but soon gets tiresome again. We now explain, "What we need now is STRATEGY (to be discussed next); we must try to find different actions each time so the other team (or a theater audience), doesn't know what to expect next." The game (or performance) is now more stimulating and has a better chance of riveting our attention. Like the Big Three, the more evenly balanced the obstacle to the objective, the more dramatic the result, whether it's a game, theater, or life. We are riveted by seeing a hero or heroine finding ways to challenge a strong obstacle to reach their desired need or goal.

Most action films, such as the Indiana Jones and James Bond films, rely on a structure of ever more insurmountable OBSTACLES for the hero to overcome. Sounds simple, but it keeps you riveted to the screen.

Obstacles are never played directly for the audience. They are for the actor. Obstacles are to be played against. Obstacles can be physical, mental, psychological, or spiritual.

Find the obstacles inherent in the script, supplied by the playwright or director. An example of a personal obstacle might be a headache or specific pain. The obstacle for Hamlet might be wrestling with his own feelings of inadequacy. For Macbeth, it might be first the King and then his conscience. A feeling of guilt, or fear of punishment by God (or another) for wrongdoings committed would prove significant obstacles. In the film *The Apartment*, Jack Lemmon has to call several people to rearrange their use of his apartment for their own personal rendezvous. This could be a dull scene, but Lemmon plays it with the obstacle of a very bad head cold (and a box of tissues) and it becomes more interesting and funny. Obstacles are as important to comedy as they are to drama.

Part 3. Actions and Strategy

The unpredictable actor, who holds your attention because you don't know what she will come up with next, is the actor who has mastered the third part of the "Big Three." What action, strategy, behavior, maneuver, move, tack, step will she apply to overcome the obstacle to what she wants?

A great piece of music or dance or other work of art will adopt a theme and deal with it in a variety of ways, or it would be boring. A boring actor or play will use little variety. An "alive" actor explores the many ways he can try to obtain an objective. If you can't get it one way, try other moves.

"Actions" are what you do to get what you want. To borrow from the military, "tactics" or actions may be roughly broken down into two main groups – those that intimidate and those that entice. "Strategy" is not necessarily devious, malicious, or unkind. The most honest person needs a plan through which to accomplish good. For example, Mahatma Gandhi would use fasting and publicity. "Strategy" is often unconscious and spontaneous. Look at your own "strategies" for getting what you want in life, and at those of others, and find the actions that your character may use. Next, look at the strategy implied – or mapped out – by the dialogue; in Shakespeare's *Othello*, Iago announces his strategy to snare Othello. Then, think of the "tactics" you can invent to give you and your character variety and interest.

An excellent example of the Big Three can be found in old silent comedies. Charlie Chaplin and Buster Keaton found many varied and inventive ways for their characters to get what they wanted. The next time you see a performance in any media, notice how the "Big Three" are handled. Observe what the characters need or want or wish, all the obstacles in their way, and all the things they do to overcome the obstacles. You can see the Big Three used throughout all good plays and films. Hamlet needs to avenge his father's death. His obstacle is his own inability to act. His strategy is to reveal his uncle's guilt by adding some words to a play he is to attend. He has at last a plan of action.

Some threatening tactics are to: flex your muscles; make yourself bigger or louder; smirk or sneer at the person; be cool or menacing; throw things; pound, grab, bluff, snarl, bully, or work on the other character's weakness or conscience. A few enticing/seducing tactics are to: smile, approve, nod, laugh with the other character, speak softly, purr, flatter, flirt, cajole, touch, hug, wheedle, coax, beg. The choice of "strategy" reveals character – where a bully might use force, for example, a pacifist would use non–aggressive means. All actions must be justified. How you carry out the actions depends on the circumstances given by the playwright.

EXERCISE

The Big Three Improvisation

One actor has a strong, urgent need to perform a prepared activity which presents some obstacle, such as performing a difficult or delicate repair job (fixing a broken clock, for example). He uses every strategy possible to complete the task within a prescribed time limit (obstacle) of about five minutes, and then he must leave for some specific reason (the bank will close, or the like).

Another actor approaches him with a very strong, urgent need that can only be fulfilled by the first actor. The first actor has to find a believable reason to refuse this need (when someone says "No," drama usually occurs. The second actor must then use as many actions and strategies as possible to get his needs met within the predetermined time limit (obstacle) of about five minutes. The exercise ends when time limits are reached. Everything must have a reason; both actors must have justifications for their actions. They come into the scene only knowing their relationship and their location. Everything else is improvised in the now.

BREAKING DOWN AND MEMORIZING THE SCRIPT

Acting is shaping your own real experiences to fulfill the obligations of the imaginary play and the characters.

A full-length script can seem formidable, but as you break it down into smaller pieces, it becomes more manageable. The best way of breaking it down is to use the "Big Three" (Tool #8) as your guide. Every time a need sets in, a new beat begins, linked to obstacles and actions. When you either fulfill or fail to fulfill that need, the beat ends and a new need sets in, and so on till the end. Do this for shape. For content, break the script down into experiences (Tool #5), which suggests you use the essences of real experiences from your life. The script will break down differently for each character.

A symphony is broken down into sections or movements; each may have its own name and beat. When you break a script down into sections, give each its own beat, and a short, descriptive name. These names should set the emotional tone for the section and will help trigger your memory. When ready, break each section down even further into "moments" (discussed later). Be very familiar with the general content of each section before you try to memorize the lines. Don't begin with "word by word" memorization because then if you miss one word, the whole piece falls apart. Learn context and content first. Start by reading the whole speech several times until you can give the general content by memory in your own words. You can then get more and more specific. Eventually, of course, you must learn it accurately. But if you know the overall sweep, you should never be completely lost. Learn thoughts – not lines! Learn the thoughts that form the lines.

You can work out your own notations for breaking down your script. Note the individual sections in the margin of the script or have a blank piece of paper opposite the text and make notes there. You can draw a line with a ruler across the whole page to indicate the separations of beats. Use pencil where you can so you can erase and change it if needed. At the top of each beat, write the need or intention for that beat, using an active verb with the word "to" before it. Then write the obstacles and the strategy or actions you will take to overcome that obstacle.

Most important of all is to break the script down into experiences (Tool #5). Find a word or two that encapsulates and will remind you of the experience you need. For example, "divorce," "hospital," "break up," and so forth. Entitle each section you have identified. Note the personalizations being used (Tool #6). Other useful tools yet to come are #11, 13, 14, and 15.

At this point it is helpful to get an overview of the play you are working on. Tell the story in as few words as possible, being careful not to over-intellectualize. For instance, the given circumstances for *Othello* by Shakespeare are: Othello, an army general, promotes Cassio to be his lieutenant over Iago, a more experienced officer who thought he rightly deserved the post. Iago plots revenge on both by falsely insinuating an affair between Cassio and Othello's virtuous wife, Desdemona.

He succeeds, causing a tragic end.

The story for the actor under the playwright's given cir-cumstances is often called "the event," or inner monologue. The event for Iago might be "I am furious. I hate that black Moor Othello. How dare he pass me over in favor of that ninny, Cassio? Am I now supposed to take orders from that ass? Never! I have a plan that will get rid of both in one fatal blow!"

Each actor would break down only his own part. I broke down the following one beat for the character of Iago. How you break it down will be very personal.

SCRIPT BREAKDOWN

Othello by William Shakespeare
ACT THREE, SCENE THREE

THEME – Jealousy aroused feeds on itself.

SPINE – Evil is as evil does. Great ones have a great fall.

SPACE – Out of doors, before the Castle.

SENSORY – Distant sounds of soldiers drilling, marching music.

OVERALL OBJECTIVE – To taste the sweetness of revenge.

THE BREAKDOWN

Character – IAGO

NEEDS – To manipulate, destroy, emasculate

OBSTACLES– Political and personal strength of Othello

ACTIONS – Pretend helpfulness& loyalty

EXPERIENCES – Mad–Fear–Glad

PERSONAL EXPERIENCE –When a director gave another actor the part I deserved

SUBTEXT – I was slighted. Iwant satisfaction.

CONDITIONS– Agitation, boredom

PERSONALIZATION – The director who gave my part
away and the other actor

MOMENTS– Enjoying Othello's squirming, appreciating
my cleverness

OPPOSITES – Disguising his fury in sweetness

NEEDS

To involve

To set the trap

To bait him

To evoke suspicion

To insinuate

To entangle

To provoke

To confuse, to torment

THE SCRIPT

IAGO. My noble Lord
OTHELLO. What dost thou say Iago
I. Did Michael Cassio when you woo'd my lady know of
   your love
O. He did from first to last why dost thou ask
I. But for a satisfaction of my thought no further harm

O. Why of thy thought Iago

I. I did not think he had been acquainted with her

O. O yes and went between us very oft.

I. Indeed.

O. Indeed ay indeed discern'st thou aught in that Is he not honest

I. Honest my Lord

O. Honest ay honest

I. My lord for aught I know

O. What doest thou think

I. Think my lord

Moments, Thoughts, & Silence

To break the script down further, divide the script into "moments." Moments are short pieces of time within the beats when the character's thoughts may search, shift, or stall. A whole beat may have many "moments" or thoughts within it.

One of the major problems for an actor is that although the playwright has already done the work of forming thoughts for him, it must appear as if he is creating them from moment to moment. Pedestrian actors will rattle off these thoughts in a steady stream. The characters they play, however, have to go through a process to earn those thoughts. Pay attention to the way you form your own thoughts and observe others. Try to get inside your characters' heads and think the way they do. Actors invariably seem to know what they are going to say in advance, while the characters do not (they have no read or memorized the play).

Practice coming to a complete stop after each thought, as if the curtain had dropped and the play is over. Then, as if the curtain rises, the next thought is formed. Our lives are really lived one "moment" at a time. This may happen very rapidly.

While you don't want to run everything together without thought, you don't want to hesitate and grope for every line either. In the end, it depends on how your character's mind works. Try to find a happy balance.

EXERCISE

For Moments

Pantomime opening a new pack of cigarettes, taking one out, putting it between your lips, opening a book of matches, taking one out, striking it, lighting the cigarette, taking a few puffs.

Now, repeat the same actions. This time, however, stop dead and be completely relaxed for a few seconds after each new movement. For example, reach for the pack, STOP. Pull it toward you, STOP. Take hold of the cellophane zipper, STOP. Slowly pull the tab around the pack, STOP. Keep doing this after the slightest new move until completion.

Then, repeat the pantomime without the actual "stops" but being just as careful with each movement. You will see quite a difference from the way you pantomimed the sequence the first time as each movement or moment is specific and clear. If you don't smoke, try it with putting on makeup or some other small task.

Our acting – and our lives – could be just as specific and clear if we learn to go from moment to moment. Try it with a scene in rehearsal.

The value of breaking down a script was brought home to me when I worked with Elia Kazan on a project of *The Oresteia* at the Actors Studio. He is a master at going right to the heart of whatever character or script you are breaking down. This lesson was reinforced when I worked with Burgess Meredith while he was preparing *Ulysses in Nighttown* for Broadway (a play I had directed Off-Broadway for the Equity Library Theater, so I knew it well). Burgess was very meticulous in his breakdown of a script. From Kazan and Burgess, I got the importance of an in-depth breakdown of the material you are working on in preparation for performing it as a director or actor. Breakdowns force you to look at your character in depth each moment and to give the whole a shape and clarity. The director breaks down all the characters in the script.

TOOL #10

PREPARATION

Decide how you want theatre to be for you; then do what has to be done.

Most performers in the performing arts and sports prepare or warm up before they perform. Actors, for the most part, seem reluctant or embarrassed to do this, and that's too bad. Their work is so much better when they do. I have been to performances where the actors didn't get warmed up until the third act. I felt cheated. I had paid for the full evening.

Preparation is especially important for film acting where an actor may have to show up in the early morning and jump into a highly charged scene.

To find the best preparation for whatever you're working on, ask, "What condition – physically, mentally, psychologically, spiritually – is the character in before and during this scene?" Then ask, "Am I now in that condition?" If not, then ask, "What do I need to do to get to that state?"

You can be very creative and inventive in getting to the condition that the character is in. There are no restrictions or rules. What works for you personally is right and may have no relation to what works for someone else, and each time you work, it may be different. Try everything, without self-censorship, until you start to find the kinds of things that work best for you.

EXERCISES

Preparation for getting to the condition the character is in before performing.

Some people are strongly affected by different kinds of music. Movies use music to evoke specific moods in the audience. Actors can use music to evoke feelings for a scene. Before rehearsing, experiment to find what music moves you for specific scenes. Have a portable cassette player and earphones handy and play some piece of music that stimulates in you the emotion needed for the scene, or hear the music in your head. Many like to use the personalization tool (#5) and "talk" to a meaningful person from their life that brings up the specific feelings that the scene calls for. It's good to combine personalization with doing something physical. Strong physical movement enhances the feelings for the scene. It's always best to do it vocally, at as great a volume as practicable. Full vocal energy will release any inhibited feelings. If this is not appropriate, do it semi–audibly, so only you can hear it. I have a single mattress standing upright against a wall that people can substitute for someone and punch and kick, or hug and caress. If you don't have a mattress, you can use the air. In a theater or studio, I look for a private space where I can prepare. If there is nowhere else, I will use the bathroom to prepare.

When talking imaginatively to a meaningful person from your life such as your parents at some specific time, you do not have to repeat what you said or did. Even more dramatic and meaningful can be to say what you did not say at the time, what was inside you. What you could, or should, or wished you had said is often more true to the essence of what happened than what you actually said or did. Say this out loud or semi–audibly. You are ready to do the play when you feel the way the character does in the play. Rarely is the scene richer or fuller than your preparation for it!

Bruce Dern, a long–time student of mine, really got a great deal from preparation. In his first Broadway play, O'Casey's *Shadow of a Gunman*, he had a scene where he was being chased offstage by British soldiers. He came onstage to leave a suitcase with friends. The audience must remember the incident later in the play when the soldiers are searching his friend's house. First of all Bruce did a great deal of work on his character. Bruce is a very diligent actor and worked on all the tools. On performance night he would also "prep" before going on. Bruce would leave the stage door, run completely around the block, and arrive backstage just before his entrance. While running, he would think, "Suppose I get mugged? What will happen if a policemen thinks I'm running from a crime and stops me? Suppose they block off the street for some reason?" He did this to create in himself a panicky state of mind. When he entered, breathless and disheveled, you believed he was being chased for his life. This outer "prep" worked so well because he did his inner work first. The audience remembered and so did the critics. He got great notices and it helped launch his career. If you do your preparation fully and faithfully, eventually you will need less and less time to get the exact result you want. Remember, your acting will be no better than your preparation. The preparation is to help you achieve the condition the character is in. It is not a substitution for the other work an actor does.

TOOL #11

NEUTRALIZING AND ACTUALIZING THE ACIING SPACE

You cannot really imagine anything you have not experienced in essence.

The space we are in – the room, the environment – affects everything we experience. Imagine the same scene taking place in a cathedral, a brothel, a forest or meadow, and a hostile jungle. All would be different simply because the space is different. For the stage actor, the environment is usually designed and built of wood, canvas, and other materials. It is an artificially created ambience for the play and the audience. For the "living character" in the imaginary play, the space is real and has an effect on him and everyone around him. In the play *A Streetcar Named Desire*, Blanche is strongly affected by the poor, noisy, dirty French Quarter of New Orleans where her sister Stella lives. The expansive space of western films stands in contrast to the lonely space with a single tree in Samuel Beckett's *Waiting for Godot*, a production I directed with Bruce Dern at the Academy of Music in Philadelphia.

Neutralize the artificial space by mentally replacing it with a real, meaningful place, since the imaginary space does not, for you, have the meaning it does for the character in the play. If the scene takes place in the great outdoors and the theatre setting is filled with artificial trees and shrubs, you may want to substitute a favorite country scene you know to make it real for you.

First ask, "How does my character experience this environment?" It will help to start with the sad, mad, glad, or afraid guide. Once you have the answer as to how it affects your character, ask yourself, "When in my life have I, in essence, experienced a place in the same way?" Sometimes you can use the parallel environment from your "experience" tool, if it fits (Tool #5).

Start working with the tool of "place" early in rehearsals, when you probably won't yet have a set. It's a good tool to use in the rehearsal studio where you can use it in place of a full set. Without a real space, your active imagination is in limbo. If you don't know where you are, you don't fully know who you are. Think about how you react when you awake in a strange place. Until you locate yourself and adjust, you don't really know fully who you are.

Be aware in your life of different places and environments and how they affect you and those around you. This will help you be aware of how important the surroundings are to your acting. How do you feel jumping waves in the ocean compared to being in an overcrowded elevator?

EXERCISES

The Acting Space

Before you work on a new set, explore the space thoroughly by using every piece of furniture in as many creative ways as possible. Use the floor; sit, lean, perch, and kneel on everything. Marlon Brando is reported to have spent the night in Stanley's stage apartment before opening in A Streetcar Named Desire on Broadway. Shelley Winters scrubbed the floor and stocked the cupboard of her stage apartment in *A Hatful of Rain* before opening in previews.

If you come on a new stage set and it is familiar to the character, walk around it, touch and use everything. If there is a sofa, sit on it, lie on it, lounge on it, kneel on it, lean over the back of it, sit on the floor and lean against it, sit on the arms, the back, and so on. Do this with as much of the stage as you can, until you feel perfectly at ease and at home.

EXERCISE

Meaningful Room

To realize and practice the power and influence of environments, try the following exercise. Fully relive being in a meaningful room, such as your childhood bedroom. Or you may pick a specific room in a house you visited that was significant for you, such as your grandparents' house, or perhaps a summer place or camp where your family stayed when vacationing.

Relive being in this meaningful room and notice what first attracts your attention in that space. Examine it in great detail. From there go in one direction around the entire room. If you come to a piece of furniture with drawers, go through each one and particularize each object to make it more real for you and possibly to bring up feelings. Go through any closets you come upon. Are there any hiding places for private things that may still stimulate your emotions? Go all the way around the walls until you come to the object you started with. See the view from each window. See the ceiling and the floor in detail; look under the bed. Then, using your senses, hear the sounds from inside and outside the room. Smell the room, taste the things you ate and drank there, touch things. Let feelings, sensations, memories come to the surface. When you are more "there" than "here" say your lines from the scene or play you are working on at present and associate them with the place where the scene takes place in the imaginary script.

You are examining a room in great detail in this exercise to show how easily you can relive a significant place from your past to bring up present feelings and emotions if you need to make the imaginary stage setting real for you.

Make associations between the words of the play and the appropriate feelings of the character for a setting. Ideally, later on, if you have properly associated words and feelings, by merely saying the words of the play the appropriate feelings will surface. The set, the character, and the script all have specific meaning for the audience through the actor. The scene designer supplies the physical setting and the actor gives it dramatic meaning and integrity.

By place, I don't mean the scenery or setting that the scene designer has supplied, but where you are as a character and how it affects you, which gives the set a personal significance for you and, through you, to the audience.

Films will usually go to great lengths and expense to find locations to provide a real place. On the stage, we have to create that environment. It's up to you to create the setting for yourself; the stage designer is working more for the audience. When the actor applies his make-up and dons his costume, the actor allows himself to be enveloped by his new environment to find himself subtly transforming into the character.

LAYERING EMOTIONS

Don't act your emotions — have the emotions and get on with what's next.

An emotion is rarely one pure, unadulterated feeling. Real-life emotions are not one-dimensionally sad, glad, mad, or fearful. Anger, for instance, may very well contain fear and sadness, and even a dose of gladness may be mixed in: there may be fear of losing control, of negative results, of retaliation, or other responses. There may be sadness from memories of someone angry at you, or that you see hurt in the other. You might be glad to get it off your chest, or pleased with your strength. The more facets there are to a feeling on stage, the more interesting, dramatic, and believable it will prove. Each emotion will have its own particular mix of feelings, even though one may dominate. To find this emotional mix, apply the useful tool of "layering."

You will see this emotional dimension in any good play or film. Watch Robert DeNiro in the film *Cape Fear*. You will see layered all possible feelings. Gentle with the young girl, cruel with her father, lecherous with the mother, threatening, clever with the law. Each facet of his behavior is a separate layer of his whole character.

Take the emotion you are working on and break it down into its many facets; then layer these aspects, one emotional layer at a time.

How you work on this will become clear in the following exercise.

EXERCISE

Layering

Ask, as in Tool #5, what the character is experiencing using the sad, mad, glad, afraid index and then name the applicable emotions in order of their dominance. Now, working backward, take the least dominant feeling first and emphasize that feeling as if it were the only feeling. For instance, if the least dominant feeling is fear, work the material as if fear were the only appropriate feeling and speak all of the words using only the fear element of the emotion. It's quite possible that many of the words won't feel right when you say them using only fear. Trust the tool for now. You may also find that there is more fear in the piece than you thought at first. Now take the next least-dominant emotion; if it's glad, work the material as if it was exclusively glad and see what you discover. Then experiment with the next feeling in the same way, saving the most dominant feeling until last. Now repeat the material one more time, and this time, let the different feelings filter in naturally. You will find that the material resonates with more subtle power. Actors I have worked with, such as Sandy Dennis and Bruce Dern, have found "layering in" different feelings in this manner very rewarding and that their work had more color, depth, interest, contrast, and authenticity. In *A Streetcar Named Desire*, Marlon Brando layers in almost all human emotions. The

Process and exercises mentioned above will demonstrate a way of accomplishing this.

Always associate the feelings with the words. You may also layer other behaviors, as in "Overall Conditions" (Tool #15 below). I was once in the play *The Petrified Forest* by Robert E. Sherwood with Jason Robards. He played his character angrily. In one scene he would slap my face and my glasses would fly off. Later, he decided his character was not that angry and the slap turned into a light tap. The layer of anger was still there but he added a layer of glad to it. As usual, he was right and the scene played much better.

TOOL #13

SILENT SUBTEXT AND FANTASY

The great actor learns to tap the reality that lies beneath the apparent reality.

So many actors think acting is only about the "words." Naturally, the words are important, but the words are just the tip of the iceberg. Special actors give you the impression that words are inadequate to express all that they feel. An example of this is seen in the film _The Piano_, in which the lead character, Holly Hunter, uses no words but communicates a great deal by her inner work. Another example is Anthony Hopkins, who, in the film _The Remains of the Day_, says very little, but whose silent subtext and inner work reveals his character's feelings and thoughts. Both actors silently express a great deal with their eyes. Silent subtext is extremely important in many contemporary works, such as plays by Samuel Beckett and Harold Pinter. As much is unsaid or intimated as is said; they both make use of the filled pause, where there is important mental and emotional life.

Most bad acting is the result of actors coming directly from the mind. They short–circuit the rest of the full–body systems. They try to ignore the sensory and vital visceral makeup of the whole person that can give your acting vitality. The nervous system, the endocrine and other systems are involved in full–body acting. This happens because in stage life, the actor is given the end result by the playwright of what would be a complicated process in real life. The playwright supplies the text, the actor must supply the sub-text.

The head is active with thoughts all the time, even when you sleep. There are thoughts that help your acting and thoughts that hurt your acting. One way to help make your acting real is to develop as many real character thoughts, actions, and feelings as possible around the words. Develop a stream of consciousness of your own, as the character, running through the words of the playwright, as it does in life with your own words. Less–believable actors have technical "actor thoughts," such as "What's my next line," "The audience seems restless," "I want to get a big laugh," "I did or did not do that line well." They are trying to act and listen to themselves at the same time, to be the actor and the audience simultaneously. Whenever you hear yourself on stage, you are not doing your best work and you'd better get back to character subtext. An example of character thoughts might be, "He's not telling the truth," "I feel so good when I'm with you," "I'm afraid you'll hurt me," "Please notice me for who I am."

Ingrid Bergman was an actress who always had a silent subtext underlying her work. In the film *Casablanca*, you were as aware of her thoughts and feelings as if she had spoken them. Greta Garbo was also famous for this quality in all her films.

Be conscious of how, in your own life, there is a constant inner monologue going on. Try to add this to all your characters. Even though it's silent, the audience will "hear" it, and often this is the more interesting drama. This technique works especially well in film, where the camera seems to pick up your inner thoughts. In film, thoughts can often be louder than words.

Our experiences, in general, can be broken down into three kinds of awareness. One is the sensory awareness of the outside: what I now actually see, hear, smell, taste, and touch. The second is awareness of the inside: what I now actually sense from inside me, feelings, emotions, discomfort, well-being, physical manifestations, and so on. The third part is awareness of fantasy activity.

Any imaginary picture existing only in mind is a fantasy. In our everyday life, we use fantasy constantly. In theatre, fantasy adds dimension and authenticity. A silent fantasy inner life goes on in our heads, almost all the time. These fantasies on stage can be a combination of character fantasies and your real fantasies about your partner and the play. They may be about almost anything – sex, grandeur, interpretation, guess-work, planning the past or future, and so on. Fantasy is the free play of the creative imagination. Fantasy incorporated in your acting comedy or drama can add a layer of richness. Cary Grant used fantasy well. You will see it in the twinkle of his eyes.

EXERCISE

For Silent Subtext

The subtext is all that is going on under and around the text. While working on the script alone you can talk out the silent thoughts about the inner life of your character, semi-audibly. While listening in rehearsals continue to talk "silently." It can add new dimensions to your acting. Silent subtext is especially effective in film, where thinking pays great dividends. This seems to be a secret of some film superstars such as Gary Cooper, Greta Garbo, Jimmy Stewart, and Ingrid Bergman. Watch for this the next opportunity you get to see one of their films. The more inner work actors do, the less outer work or overacting they do. Silent film stars had to learn this skill of necessity. Overdone it could be disastrous. Charlie Chaplin could express his inner work expertly and it communicated nonverbally through his expressions and his body language.

EXERCISE

For Fantasy

Sometimes, after a scene, I ask the actors to pick some secret fantasy about their partner as characters or in life. They need never reveal the fantasy. They do the scene a second time with awareness of this fantasy beneath everything they do. The scene then invariably has a definite richness that it did not have before. Develop real character thoughts and fantasies around, in between, and on, the words that the playwright has given you while doing the scene to give it a richness.

Since we are discussing the importance of the mind and inner work of the actor, let's talk about what is perhaps one of the greatest destroyers of natural talent – negative and self-defeating thoughts. These negative thoughts are especially toxic if experienced while you are acting. One remedy for this self- defeating habit is to keep a healthy subtext or inner character monologue going so there is no room for negative or judgmental thoughts to come through.

TOOL #14

EXPLORING OTHER ACTING POSSIBILITIES

CONSIDERING THE OPPOSITE

Nature is much more than what appears on the surface.

So many things in life seem to contain their opposite and that's what makes them dramatic. It's the shadows that make the highlights vibrant; day and night, tide in and tide out, the changing seasons, life and death, and so on. This aspect of nature is too often omitted from acting. When the opposite is incorporated by an actor, it can give a rewarding dimension that otherwise would be missing. Opposites attract the audience.

Ultimately you want to be able to integrate the opposites so that you are not bound by either. You can then go to a new creative place, the interweaving of the opposites to the mix you want.

EXERCISE
Opposites

Write down what seems obvious about your character, and then, in rehearsal, try experimenting with being the opposite; in performance, blend both. You can't lose; even if you decide against it, you will be giving your character dimension and color. You will stretch yourself, and many times you will find the opposite quality is a more exciting choice. The more facets a diamond has, the more brilliant it is; the same goes for acting, and for most aspects of theater and life.

Marlon Brando knows how to play the opposites very well. In *The Godfather Part One*, Brando's character has people murdered, and yet with his own children and grandchildren we see him being gentle and even playful. In *On the Waterfront*, Brando is a rough fighter, and yet in scenes with Eva Marie Saint he is sensitive and tender. In *A Streetcar Named Desire*, he gets violently drunk, fights, and throws the radio out the window. A little later, he cries his famous, "STELLA!!" and says, "I want my girl down here," like a little boy. Later, we see him roughly rape Blanche, and at the end he is penitent and humble. He shows us two believable opposite sides of the same character. In John Steinbeck's *Of Mice and Men*, at the McCarter Theatre, I played opposite John Lithgow. He played Lenny and caught beautifully both sides of his character; gentle as a lamb one time and strong as a bear another time.

Find the toughness in a weak character, and the weakness in a tough character. Look for the good in the bad, and vice versa. Just look at yourself and the people around you and notice how many different dimensions are there. For dramatic values, interest, and truth, always consider the opposite in your roles, and then choose what mix you want. Rehearsals are for exploring. Too many actors and directors use this time to set things, and it becomes rote and mechanical. Rehearsals can be an exciting adventure for examining possibilities. Average actors work in rehearsals to find comfort. They do the same thing over and over, trying to make it "safe" for themselves, and they succeed only in making it dull and mechanical, devoid of life and spontaneity. Rehearsal is an opportunity to explore the edge, to see how far you can go. Go all the way to the edge, but not over it. Usually the edge is farther along than you imagined. You can't go wrong in rehearsal, because you can always pull back if the director thinks it's too much, but the stretch itself is rewarding. For example, you invariably feel actors such as Robert DeNiro, Al Pacino, Glenn Close, Dustin Hoffman, and Bruce Dern know how to play close to the edge, taking risks with themselves.

I once learned a great acting lesson from a dog. I worked in a summer theater in New Hampshire; the producer's house was nearby. Her dog roamed the theater by day but had to be locked in her basement by night to prevent him from roaming onstage. One night, he hid out at showtime, and although everyone was watching out for him, he showed up onstage in the middle of Act Two. Well, we actors could act our hearts out; the audience was interested only in the dog. He stole the show because the dog was the only one onstage that night who was really spontaneous, unrehearsed, unpretentious, totally in the "now," real, and, above all, unpredictable!

I rarely see that open, fresh quality in an actor. Once, I saw a preview of *The Immortalist* by Ruth and Augustus Goetz. We in the audience came alive when a young actor walked onstage in the middle of a group. He played the non-speaking part of an Arab boy and was only onstage for a short time but the stars were forgotten. You could not take your eyes off this actor. His name meant nothing to me at the time, but later, I found out it was Jimmy Dean.

Some of my students or actors I directed had this quality — Bruce Dern, Sandy Dennis, and Judd Hirsch, among others. It's an indefinable quality of inner restlessness that leads to unpredictability. It can be acquired if you dare to march to your own inner drummer.

OBLIGATIONS AND OVERALL CONDITIONS

No acting that comes from outside ourselves or our experience is real.The script "obligates" us to particular conditions. For instance, the script indicates it's hot or cold, or we are drunk or in love. Take note of these "obligations" as the audience is quick to look for matching behaviors. Conditions can come from outside ourselves, as in N. R. Nash's play, *The Rainmaker*; the characters all talk about the temperature being 110 degrees in the shade. In *Rain*, John Colton and Clemence Randolph's adaptation of Somerset Maugham's story, the weather influences everyone's behavior in great measure. The heavy tropical rain prohibits the characters from venturing outdoors. They are locked together in the close quarters of the small hotel. The condition of the rain brings out bizarre behavior that ends in tragedy.

Some obligations come directly from the script. For example, your partner may have a line saying, "Stop yelling," or "Why did you hit me?" When breaking down the script, as in Tool #9, make note of these obligations.

Some obligations come from the inside or from a physical manifestation. The condition of Laura's being handicapped in *The Glass Menagerie* makes her feel inadequate and touches every aspect of her life. The overall condition of Cyrano De Bergerac's long nose dictates his special existence

118 ◆ ◆ ◆ ◆ ◆ ◆ ◆ ◆ ◆ ◆ *GORDON PHILLIPS*

and affects everything about his life.

If you have a severe headache or physical pain, it can influence everything about you. It can change your behavior and thinking, your attitude, even your whole personality. When you hurt, you are preoccupied and subdued. This may be something you want your character to have to cope with. Work on it by reliving a sharp pain you have experienced.

In O'Neill's A *Long Day's Journey Into Night*, Jamie is drunk most of the time the audience sees him, (for drunk, blend tools #1, 2, 3 and 5). And in the film *Rainman*, Dustin Hoffman's condition of autism makes him behave in an unusual manner at times and certainly shapes his whole life. The way to work on such overall conditions is to use sensory and emotional reliving and physical imagination, reliving times when you experienced in essence (not necessarily literally) the different aspects of the condition, as outlined in Tools #2, 3, and 5 earlier in the book.

In the film *Being There*, Peter Sellers seems to be mentally handicapped, which influences his whole way of behaving. You can work on a character like that by reliving a time when you were sick, or extremely exhausted, or even the moment of waking up from a deep sleep and feeling disoriented.

Try the condition in rehearsal to see if the result you get is what you and the director want. Different kinds and intensities of headaches, for example, will of course give different results for different people. Some other overall conditions are nausea, specific pain, great haste, time of day, need to be quiet, and depression or elation.

You can also use an overall condition to experience your character's problems. For example, if a character you are playing is under great stress, like the characters in *Oedipus the King* or *Medea*, you may choose "having a headache" to give you the preoccupied pain and intensity the character is suffering. The audience should never know you are using the condition of a headache. They will associate the pain with the character's condition.

EXERCISE

Conditions

To test the strong influence of this tool, try repeating a scene, this time adding a specific overall condition. You will be convinced of its power to change the quality of the whole scene. For instance, add nausea or a specific pain. A physical or mental problem is chosen according to the requirements of the material you are acting. Find the specific tool by trial and error in rehearsals until you and the director are satisfied.

We can work on more than one condition at the same time by building them in layers, starting with the weakest condition and ending with the strongest (much as you do with tool #13 for emotions and feelings).

THE EXPRESSIVE VOICE AND PROCESS SINGING

Singing is much like speaking, only you do it on pitch.

Certainly, voice and diction are important tools for acting. To do justice to these tools would require a separate book – and many have been written. Look at a book by Kristin Linklater entitled *Freeing the Natural Voice* (Drama Books), and a book by Edith Skinner called *Speak with Distinction* (Applause Books). I will give only a few notes. First, find the very best teacher you can. Make sure the instructor is not trying to teach you to "act" with the voice, much like an old fashioned radio actor. Practice the lessons diligently and let good voice and diction become an integral part of your everyday life. Never try to apply the lessons while you are acting, because both will suffer. If you work hard to have good voice and diction become a natural part of your daily life, then you can forget it while acting; you will "own" it naturally.

To get the greatest variety of parts, you need a relatively strong, neutral voice that is free of regional accents and other impediments to being easily heard and understood, a voice that can go in any direction that the character dictates. If the part obligates you to have an accent, regional or foreign, there are teachers, books, and tapes to help you. For accents I use a two–volume set titled *Manual of American*

Dialects and *Manual of Foreign Dialects* by Lewis and Marguerite Shalett Herman (Theater Arts Books, New York). I suggest not using an accent in your work unless you have studied it very well first, for then you "own" a good accent for the rest of your career. If you "wing it," then you suffer from an indifferent, sloppy accent all your career.

Work to have a good, clear, free, well–modulated, and expressive voice that can go in any direction you, the character, or the director chooses.

Process Singing

I've had great success with "Process Singing." Using the exact same tools that are presented in this book for acting, substitute the words of a song in place of the words of a play. Start with a song you don't know and, if possible, a song you haven't heard often. Relax (Tool #1), and without the melody, learn the words in neutral (Tool #4), then actualize the words and present them as if doing a monologue (Tool #5). Pick a personalization (Tool #6), and gradually add the melody and the rest of the tools (#8, 10, 11, 12, 13, 14, 15) as appropriate and slowly begin to work in your singing voice.

I have directed musicals and worked with individual singers using this technique and it gets great results. Even if you don't consider yourself a singer, I urge you to try it. It can be an asset to your career to be able to put across a song, and may just put you ahead of the competition.

EXERCISE

For the Expressive Voice

Open Throat and Forward Thrust Voice

The two exercises I use most often for fast results involve the use of a straight wine cork and a plastic drinking straw. Start by standing with your back completely flat against a straight wall, including your head. Put one hand on your stomach and the other on your chest. Inhaling deeply, let the hand on your stomach move outward while the other hand (the one on your chest) barely moves outward and only at the end of the breath, when the stomach and diaphragm are fully extended. After doing this fully and strongly until you are comfortable with it (for about five minutes), put a long wine cork lengthwise between your teeth; cut it down if it is too long [see illustration]. Tuck the tip of your tongue under the lower ledge of the cork against your lower teeth and leave it there, raising and lowering only the rest of your tongue. With full breathing and the tongue under the lower ledge of the cork, and with your head held straight against the wall, hold up and read aloud a short passage of something you are not interested in, maybe the editorial page of a newspaper. It will sound strange, but memorize the feeling of your open throat. Now, remove the cork and read the same passage with full breathing and clear, open throat. You will hear a deeper, richer voice that is your natural sound. If you are not sure, re-introduce the cork until you can replicate the open throat feeling that you can get with the cork between your teeth and full projection.

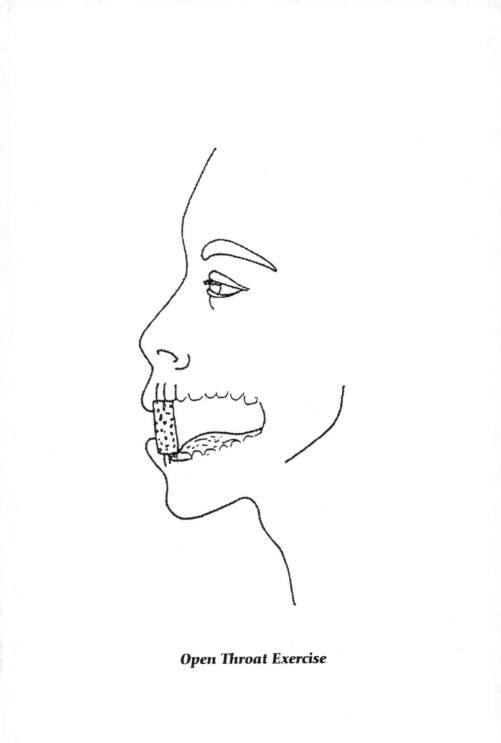

Open Throat Exercise

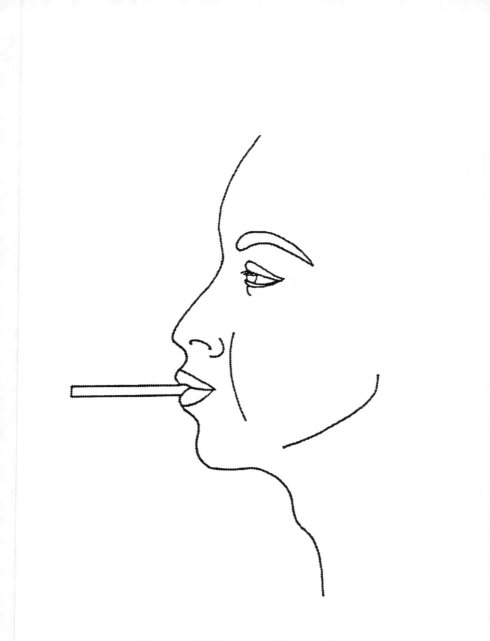

Forward Thrust and Projection

To bring the voice forward and out, use the straw. Place a plastic straw tightly between your lips, and breathe fully through it [see illustration]. Imagine that the other end of the straw extends to the back of a theatre. Next, read the same passage through the straw. Memorize the feeling, then remove the straw and with the open throat of the cork exercise, and full breathing from the stomach, speak forward and fully outward as if still using the straw. The exercises will feel and sound strange, but we are after the feeling of the open throat and forward thrust of the words. You will like the sound of your new, richer voice. Practice it until you own it naturally with both your everyday and theatre voices.

Occasionally, an actor will do good, honest, inner work, but because she has worked diligently with a "wrong" voice and diction teacher (one who encourages an affected voice, or teaches acting using the voice alone), the actress comes across as dishonest or artificial. Wrong teachers can be recognized by their own phony-sounding voices. Sometimes, it is better to work with a good singing teacher (one who will help you find your own natural voice) than a "bad" voice and diction teacher. You can usually find a good voice teacher if you search using recommendations, asking people whose voices you like who they study with, or trial and error.

Projection of your voice through the whole theater is extremely important, as is clear diction. You must, at least, be seen and heard. In production, have the director test your voice for volume and clarity from the last row while he rattles programs, shuffles his feet, coughs and clears his throat loudly, all of which the audience will do.

Opera and Acting

Stanislavski loved opera and worked diligently to raise the level of acting in opera. One major fear seems to be that if the singer gets emotional he may lose some vocal control. What I have found is that if you learn to act well and learn to sing well at the same time you can discover how to blend the two. If you can condition your vocal and acting instruments naturally then they will, without extra concentration, serve you when you sing

I have worked with opera singers at Yale University and the Curtis Institute of Music with great effect. As the singer's life gets integrated into their vocal apparatus and the emotional part of the brain gets stimulated, the color and timbre of the voice gets richer. I may use arias instead of monologues and recitative for scenes. We start in neutral and work through all the corresponding tools for acting. The noted opera director and coach, Kay Walker Castaldo, states that she gets great results working the "The Process" in all her operas.

STAGE MOVEMENT AND THE BODY AS AN EXPRESSIVE INSTURMENT"

If the body is allowed to deteriorate, the whole brain-body system will follow.

What follows is an advanced treatment of "Physical Reliving" (Tool #3). Tool #3 stresses the imaginary body; this tool deals more with the real body.

Acting is the outer expression of the inner life of the character. Along with the voice, the actor's body is the most important tool for the outer expression of his inner life. Ideally, every move the actor makes would come from the character's center of being. Any good dancer knows and practices this principle in all her work. If the movement in a play is not right, or feels awkward, then, most likely, it is not connected to the inner life of the character, or else the intention or strong "need" is not clear (Tool #8).

The body is inextricably involved in all our feelings and emotions. You can't imagine crying or laughing without the body being involved in some way. If your body is inhibited, your acting will be inhibited. All the feelings you hold in and don't express, from any part of your life, get locked in your body, cut off from full expression. We work to free the body in order to free our acting.

You can't write adequately about movement; you have to experience it. Just about all the physical disciplines can be helpful. You are more likely to stick to something you like. Take modern dance classes which explore the whole body expressively, (not ballet in the beginning; it can be a bit rigid). Fencing, karate, yoga, and active sports are all useful. Some actors find body disciplines such as Lowen's "Bioenergetics," the "Alexander Technique," and "Rolfing" very valuable. Explore them all firsthand with a qualified teacher. There are also books on these disciplines if a teacher is not available.

EXERCISES

For Body Expression

Movement with Feeling

Start by neutralizing the body as much as possible. Stand and balance your head over your neck and the neck over your shoulders and top of your spine, the shoulders over the chest, and keep working down to your feet on the floor and then up to your head again. Try to balance each part of the body so well that you feel you could stand comfortably without effort for a long time. Then, slowly move each part of the body, one at a time, and explore the flexibility of each part. Give sound to the feelings each body part evokes as you move it, using the vowel sounds. Trust the sounds that emerge. Sometimes they release pent-up emotions and repressed pain. Then start to move forward with the whole body a few steps, pause, and then move backward. Start to

make the forward movement more aggressive, add aggressive sounds, and get MAD. Try thrusting out your arms with
strong sounds at the same time. After a pause, as you move
backward, let the body feel and express FEAR with sound.
Hold out your arms, palms facing out, as if fending something off. After a pause, let the body move upward and feel
GLAD, while sounding the emotion. Thrust your arms out
and up. Then move downward in a crouch and let yourself
feel SAD, adding sounds. Curl up your fingers and bring
your fists close to your body. Move left and right to shade
or modify the feelings. For instance, forward and right is
less angry because it is not as direct. Being direct is stronger.

We primarily move in these six directions: forward, back,
up, down, right and left. Explore them with feeling and
sound. Then, use combinations of these six directions.
Choose a character and explore the movement pattern that
expresses the inner life of that character. King Richard III,
by Shakespeare, is deformed and may move like a crab –
sideways. A character like Portia in *The Merchant of Venice* may
move in straight lines because she is direct. Rosalind in *As
You Like It* may walk upward or lightly because she is
sprightly. Have fun moving and expressing feelings with
your whole body. You can especially see this type of movement in good dancers and dance groups like Martha
Graham and Alvin Ailey. Actors can benefit by studying
with a good dance teacher or movement group.

MORE EXERCISES

For Body Expression, Body Freedom

A good exercise for loosening a tight body is to make exag-
gerated gestures and movements for just about every word
you say. Go all out! It's even O.K. to ham it up, especially
for someone shy and physically uptight. Break that inhibiting armor!

Another exercise is to fully imitate a wild and crazy popular comedian or rock star. Be Phyllis Diller, Steve Martin,
Jerry Lewis, Elvis, or be Michael Jackson or Mick Jagger, or
anyone physically loose and free. To be emotionally alive –
you must be physically   alive!   Don't impose thought
between the impulse and the movements.

You may ask, "How am I going to manage all these different
tools when I have one play or scene to deal with? Let me
use a landscape painting to illustrate. I look at the painting
as a whole, and I see there is foreground and background.
Actually, whatever I concentrate on becomes foreground for
me, and everything else becomes background to it for the
moment. I can go over the whole painting this way, seeing
foreground, background, foreground, background. It's the
same with the tools. The actor goes from tool to tool as
needed, never losing awareness of the whole. Use only the
tools you need when and where you need them. They will
lead you on the pathway to "higher acting." If you learn and
practice all the tools well, they will filter in at the right time
and place.

PART TWO

USING THE TOOLS IN A ROLE

CHARACTER CREATION

INNER FACETS OF SELF

***The character is a real human being created out of the
material of another real human being — the actor.***

Don't think of "character" as something you put on from the
outside, like someone else's coat. It rarely fits you that way.
Character is something you create out of your own being,
from the many facets of your own nature.

To use a scientific analogy, Dr. Rupert Sheldrake, an emi-
nent biologist and biochemist, was recently interviewed on
PBS and he said that "genetically we are all the same and at
the same time unique." Within each of us there are the
potential characteristics of all of us. Within each of us is the
full gamut of human traits. We each have the potential for
every aspect of behavior from the most intense cruelty to
the most altruistic thoughts and acts. It is well–document-
ed that soldiers could cruelly torture human beings by day
and in the evening attend a concert or ballet and play gently with their children. We can be devils and saints, and
everything in between, and beyond. You don't have to go
outside of yourself to find any character you want or need
to play. True, there is a range within which you will feel
more comfortable. A standard piano has eighty–eight keys,
but you can play in an indeterminable number of styles –
everything from classic to contemporary – by selecting the

right combination of keys and techniques. The human being has thousands of "keys" to play on, all of which will be accessible to the actor who has developed his or her full range.

It is my personal observation from acting, directing and teaching that some actors stay outside the script because it's painful to go inside. Often, these same actors stay on the surface of their own lives. They never explore the rich depths of all that they can be.

Many people utilize only a small part of their potential flexibility. We need to explore our dark side as well as our light side, to accept the habitually disowned, unacceptable, and shadow parts of ourselves. We are generally afraid of the dark, but these realms are very dramatic, and so are the dark aspects of our nature. The actor works for a balance of all the human qualities. You need the ability to pull out and play any of the parts of yourself as if each were all of you. The versatile actor can then mix these parts in any combination desired. You can magnify or suppress the smallest quality of yourself.

You may learn a great deal about your character by noting what other characters in the play say about him or her. If you play an unsavory character, find as many positive and likeable qualities about the character as possible. The actor must learn to believe in his or her character, even if playing a Hitler. (See Considering the Opposite, Tool #14).

If ever you have to play a character that behaves in a way that you feel you never could, perhaps a murderer or a prostitute, ask yourself, "What would have to happen to me for me to behave like this character?" Most of us have prostituted ourselves in some way at some time. Haven't you had the feeling of almost wanting to kill a child molester or a deliberately cruel person? We never play ourselves per se. We play out of ourselves, facets of ourselves, which is quite different than playing ourselves as ourselves.

DO NOT say "What would I do in this situation?" Say instead, "What about me would have to change physically, mentally, psychologically, spiritually, etc. for me to behave as this character does?"

It's important to find the conscious or unconscious "skeleton" of the role or character. Find the vital spine or soul or key to unlock that part for you, something to support or hang the part on as a whole. This can be anything that works for you. A piece of inspiring music, a poem, a song, a dance. The "armature" or "skeleton" for the actor playing Oedipus is to find the truth at any cost.

In theater, we say we have a "part" in a play; we say we are playing a "part." Think of your role as playing a "part" of yourself, any part you choose of the many possibilities.

When one of my actors claims to have a headache or a cold, I tell them, "You mean the character is sick tonight." If you put it on the character, it takes the strain off you. After all, characters, to you, are living beings and are susceptible to everything you are. It's a bit like the stories where an alien comes down and takes over the body of a human. The character takes over your body, including your mind, and lives through you.

EXERCISE

Stepping into Character

In Tool #3, we worked on Physical Reliving, the "imaginary body." Try creating an imaginary image of yourself a short distance in front of the real you. Now step into that imaginary you with your real body; feel what it's like, and, when ready, step back into the real you. Step back and forth between the two until you are comfortable with it. Next, in front of you, create, in great detail, an imaginary character you are working on. When ready, step into the character, "try it on for size"; if it doesn't fit your image, keep adjusting, and stepping back and forth until it does. When satisfied, move around as that character. Experiment with it. (You can refer back to Tool #3 for guidance if needed)

EXERCISE

For Character

Animal Substitution

I imagine the earliest "actors" in human history were those who put on the "costume" of an animal's skin and, in essence, became that animal. They moved, danced, or sounded like that animal, perhaps for entertainment but more likely with a deep spiritual significance. We can see similar behavior today in primitive tribes in undeveloped regions throughout the world. It's easy to imagine this ritual in ancient societies. Anthropologists such as Margaret Mead witnessed and wrote about such behaviors in modern day tribes.

We often describe people in animal terms – he's a wolf, she's foxy, wise as an owl, a rat, bearlike.

Ask yourself what animal, in essence, does your character resemble? Get "inside your animal's skin" by observing in specific detail everything about that animal. How are paws different from feet or hands? Where is the distribution of weight? Look

the animal in the eyes and try to get into their thinking. Try to observe them in all their moods and activities. Watch them feed, play, sleep and so on.

Get down on "all fours" and become that animal inside and out. Live that animal as fully as possible, including full movement and sound. Don't imitate or pretend. Be that animal. Notice the differences between you, but especially notice the similarities. There are more than you may think.

The next step is to become less and less that animal until you are left with just enough of its essence that you could walk down a busy street and not attract special attention (well, in Manhattan you might never attract attention). Now add its essence to your character. If you never use this exercise in a play, it's good for stretch.

For further study visit the zoo often, watch nature programs and videos, and read *National Geographic.*

Sid, one of my advanced students was recently struggling with the character of Gus in Pinter's *The Dumb Waiter.* He worked on and mastered the Cockney accent. The problem was that the actor is bright but the character is not. I suggested that he do the "animal exercise" described above using a bear. He went to the Central Park Zoo several times and even found a bear named Gus! He worked diligently on it and the whole character fell in place. That bear was the "spine" of the role for him, physically, mentally, in every way. The audience never knew where it came from, and they shouldn't.

When a male sperm penetrates a female egg, the chemical mixture creates a NEW being. Now, when you, the actor, and the character mix, a new being is also created out of this union, namely, the actor's living character. As in human birth, this living character is made organically out of you, now its parent. Babies and acting are not made out of your head. The average actor tries to "do it" with their head.

HOW CHARACTERS ARE CREATED

An imaginary chemical representing the playwright's unchanging character as set down (Shakespeare's Hamlet).

A different chemical representing the actor playing the role of Hamlet and subject to normal human changes.

The mixture of the playwright's imaginary fixed character and the unique actor playing the part of Hamlet is no longer strictly the playwright's Hamlet nor strictly the actor as himself, but a new creation which is the blending of both.

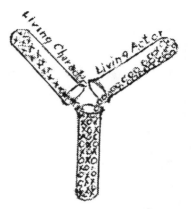

The actor does not play himself, per se, but plays out of the many facets of himself.

The mixture of actor and character creates the actor's living characte

Because the chemical representing the actor is always different – each Hamlet is always different. Never imitate – create.

– 19 –

NOTES ON PLAYING COMEDY

COMEDY IS FUNNY REALITY.

COMEDY IS SERIOUS BUSINESS AND DIFFICULT TO
WRITE ABOUT. HERE ARE A FEW NOTES ABOUT
COMEDY FOR ACTORS. THE SAME TOOLS APPLY
FOR COMEDY AS FOR DRAMA.

I have frequently asked actors in my classes to do a standard comedy scene for the first time in neutral (Tool #4), purposely avoiding all acting techniques. When the lines and situation were clever and funny, the class would be roaring with laughter. Comedy is often more about the words than about what actors do to make it funny. If it's good – trust the writing. I'm not addressing the mimes, sight gag and farcical performers as much as straight acting in straight comedy.

Most good theatre comedy is about real people in real situations that are funny. If you try to make it funny, it usually falls flat. Alfred Lunt, a great American actor, got a big laugh on a certain line in *Idiot's Delight*, by Robert Sherwood, on opening night and every night thereafter, until one night the laughs stopped coming. It stayed that way. He said to his actress wife, co-star Lynn Fontaine, "You know, that line about marriage used to get a big laugh and now, nothing."

She said, "It would if you would stop playing that line for a laugh. Sure enough, the next night he played his intention, and got his laugh back.

The character in a comedy rarely thinks his situation is funny. Usually, the more intense and serious they are, the funnier it is. Think of Woody Allen, for instance.

Comedy has a particular kind of energy. One morning at the Actors Studio, John Gielgud joined us as a guest observer. Two members were doing a comedy scene. During the feedback after the scene, I remember Sir John saying, "Playing comedy is like champagne, with bubbles rising up through the body from the feet." That hit home for me. I felt that exact feeling many times when playing comedy, but couldn't express it so succinctly.

Comedy requires more of the conscious mind than does drama. We need both our conscious and unconscious mind for acting comedy and drama, but each requires a different mix.

In general, drama is conflict. Comedy is contrast. Look at Laurel and Hardy, or Abbott and Costello – teams usually have contrasting types. Comedy is full of contrast. My favorite photograph is of Einstein sticking his tongue out fully at the camera – the contrast is evident. Comedy often has an ironical turn.

Comedy is surprise! It usually has a twist at the punch line. Comedy is more delivered than is drama. Comedy is frequently normal, everyday events – carried to the extreme.

Comedy is often a profound state of innocence. Great comedians like Charlie Chaplin knew this well. In playing comedy, look for the innocence, as with Forest Gump and many others. This applies equally to classical plays.

Comedy is a point of view, an attitude, often a slightly

oblique way of looking at things. There are many kinds of comedy. Try to get in tune with the particular style you are working on. In short, good comedy is reality that is funny.

.

20

ACTING THE CLASSICS (STYLE AND COSTUME)

THERE IS ACTING THAT IMITATES NATURE AND THEN THERE IS ACTING THAT IS NATURE.

All the basic tools given in this book fit the classics as well as they fit contemporary plays. You may need to do research to acquire a familiarity with styles of dress, behavior, speech–patterns, and other technical aspects of classical theater that you have not lived with, but your character has. There are many fine books and classes to assist you with the technical work.

Imagine an Elizabethan actor, living four hundred years ago, entering a time machine and arriving in New York today to get a job in theater or film. He would have to do the exact same work to get a part in a David Mamet play or Clint Eastwood movie that you would have to do to play Shakespeare today. Styles change but the basic work never does.

Hamlet's advice to the players (*Hamlet*, Act III, Scene 2) is as applicable today as it was then.

Like voice, diction, and body work, the classics are important for the actor to have in his tool bag. Most class-es emphasizing the classics work on valuable technical aspects: voice, diction, phrasing, metrics, gesture, movement, costume.

Actors generally harbor a fear of anything called classical. Fear can inhibit you, preventing you from doing your best work. The classics become less frightening when we look at the similarities between us and people living in other times and cultures. It's a bit like concentrating on the half–full glass rather than the half–empty. Look at the similarities on the human level. Try not to forget that well–written, so–called classical characters are human beings not unlike ourselves. Their environment may be different, but inside they basically experience everything we do. However talented, most of the playwrights, like Shakespeare, were working theater people, with the same concerns and aspirations we have.

When rehearsing the classics work with clothing approximating your costumes, so that you won't have to make a disturbing adjustment in performance. Women need to have long rehearsal skirts, petticoats, and other costume props that are floor length. The full–length skirt conditions the way your move and feel. It's quite a different feeling from wearing jeans.

Men need to feel at home in boots, hats, gloves, walking sticks, spats, ruffles, lace, glasses, full dress suits, tuxedos, and so on. These costumes and accessories can change your whole way of behaving. Often, the manners of characters are dictated by the lace and fringe dangling from their costumes, and not a general "style" or copying of others. And remember, a few hundred years from now, actors will have to study this period to play our contemporary plays.

EXERCISE

For Period Plays

Paintings

Find period paintings or pictures of paintings that to you most resemble the character and period you are working on. Go to a museum shop or library to see if they have a copy of your painting so you can rehearse with it at home. Then, working from the outside in, physicalize the pose of the character in the painting with your own body. Make it as exact as possible. Find cloth and altered clothes that generally match the painting. Use scarves, laces, curtains, and so on. Use a full–length mirror. You may want to give the copy of your picture to someone you trust for feedback. Assume the pose of the figure in the painting as accurately as you have observed and rehearsed. Slowly bring your character fully alive. Going inside yourself, use the appropriate tools to find the inner life of your creation. Working from the outside in, let the pose dictate how you move and behave. Improvise some actions or business of the period. Alter aspects of your own voice and speech to fit the character as you envision them from the painting, and speak about yourself from the character's viewpoint.

Read copies of published personal letters, diaries, and books written in the period you are working on to get an authentic feeling of the time. Effort spent researching will add richness to your acting and give you added security and authority. Researching is a valuable tool in itself. Research everything, but never let it remain in your head exclusively, or it is useless. The work must translate into action or behavior on some level.

Do your voice and diction work diligently with a good voice teacher. Don't assume a phony English accent for the classics – the accent has changed over time and a modern English accent is probably no closer to "accurate" than your own.

21

THE BUSINESS OF SHOW BUSINESS

A Good Actor Is a Bad Actor Who Never Gave Up.

FILM, TV, SOAPS

The deep internal and external work of the Process serves extremely well for acting in film and TV where the camera practically can see you think. Like a painter who switches from oil to water color, it's a matter of small adjustments from stage to film. You can pick up the technical part and terminology rather easily on your first job. I recommend that you look at a book by the film actor, Michael Caine, entitled *Acting in Film* (Applause Theatre Books).

Film can be highly technical. I remember my first full–screen close–up was shot in Europe. I was using all of the tools of acting I could, as well as I could, in my close–up. The director got a signal from the cameraman and said, "Cut." They were all looking at my feet. I looked down and saw that I was – perhaps – an inch away from my mark. I was embarrassed and it never happened again (one inch – WOW!). That's how critical the focus is on an extreme close–up. Your acting skills must really be solid to also coordinate all of the technical requirements of film. Incidentally, Michael Caine covers "hitting your mark" in his book.

The Business

Unless you have great contacts, the business of "show business" is learned the hard way, through trial and error. Get out there and ask questions of everyone. Again, there are books and guides that try to assist you. I never found any great short–cuts or secrets.

The best thing that I can wish for you is to fall in love with the process of acting, not the goal. If you fall in love with the process, you can always be happy, for that's all there is!

When you feel the time is ripe, it's a good idea to audition for everything. Even if you don't get jobs right away, it's good practice. Keep notes of what you think you could do to improve. Watch and learn from others when you can. Find a good teacher to keep growing and be ready when your day comes. Persist, but take breaks when you need them. Have fun. Don't let yourself get depressed.

You need two things: getting a break and being ready. It won't work if you have only one of them.

PART THREE

THE COMPLETED ACTOR

- 22 -

THE REASON YOU CAN ACT

The Extremely Flexible Human Being

YOU CANNOT BE MORE OF AN ACTOR THAN YOU
ARE A PERSON. YOU CANNOT GIVE WHAT YOU
DON'T HAVE.

In your dreams, when the imagination is unbounded, you can go anywhere, do anything, be anybody. When your alarm clock sounds you wake up and instantly switch to a totally different reality. You are the same person, able to easily switch between and adjust to two distinct realities, a fantastic dreaming state and a sober waking state. This is essentially what an actor does; you learn to shift consciousness from ordinary reality to imagined reality as from waking to dreaming.

One morning, you may wake from a great night's sleep feeling energetic and on top of the world. Another day, you wake depressed, lethargic, and just not wanting to face the world, and seem a completely different "character." You could easily communicate two opposite impressions to two different people meeting you for the first time on those two different occasions. Without going outside yourself you can, in essence, find all the characters you will ever need. You are always playing a part of yourself. Within each of us, there are many parts, sub–personalities. No matter how old you get, you will always have within you the sensitive, magical child you once were, as well as the shaky adolescent. You have internalized the voices and influences of parents, teachers, and significant others who helped shape you. There is your sensual, sexual part, the saint, the devil, the pusher, the perfectionist, the critic – on and on. I read that Dustin Hoffman said he got in touch with the "female" side of himself to play Tootsie. In a personal communication, a noted psychiatrist, Dr. Howard Weinberg, stated that we all carry within us both factors of male and female. All of these parts are available to all of us all the time. They are right there within us waiting to be asked to come out and play on the stage at our will. In plays like *The Mark of Zorro* or *The Scarlet Pimpernel*, the actor is called upon to play both sides of one man, first disguised as the feminine fop and then the masculine hero.

Under extreme stress, some people adapt by developing alternate personalities. The life stories of some of these people were brought to our attention in books and films such as *Sybil* and *The Three Faces of Eve*. These people seem to function as one person, but can, literally in a blink of an eye, become a completely different person. Some of their personalities will have testable symptoms, like specific allergies and other maladies, which the other "personalities" do not have. Brain wave patterns have registered differently for each of their personalities. Some of their "characters" are completely uninhibited and others are shy and retiring. Obviously, people with Multiple Personality Disorder have no choice but to splinter into these personalities, but you do. You can choose to be any person or character you want. Like surfing with the TV remote from channel to channel, actors can switch from character to character from within their whole being. You don't have to act when you can be. As always, Shakespeare said it best: "One man in his time plays many parts." I'm not saying that it's easy, only that, with work, it's possible to bring it all out of our own being.

All of us carry within us at all times the potential for every mental disability. At different times, to varying degrees, we display diverse symptoms. We all know what it's like to feel depressed, manic, compulsive, paranoid, and schizoid to some degree.

In my classes, I have done an exercise called "Marat Sade." Students take one of their own most familiar tendencies and enlarge upon it as much as possible, with control. When they all get going you would think that you were in a snake pit. The purpose of the exercise is to show how easily and safely we can become a completely different character without going outside ourselves. (Try this exercise only under proper super-vision.)

One man puts his hand inside his coat and says, "I'm Napoleon," and they put him in a padded cell. Another man does the same and they give him an Academy Award. Essentially, they are both doing the same thing. The only dif-ference is, when they say "cut," one of them can stop being Napoleon and the other cannot.

When we begin life in the womb we pass through all the stages of evolution. We start out as one cell, grow in a sealike liquid with bones resembling coral, and seem at one point more like a fish, complete with flippers which evolve into arms and fingers. Neurologist Oliver Sacks says we have rem-nants of gills. We develop a tail which gradually diminishes to the little piece we still have at the end of our spine. We all still have, as part of our brain, remnants of reptilian and early mammalian brains. In other words, we have within us a useful memory of the whole history of the universe clear back to the beginning and possibly farther, according to one of the most important paleontologists of our time, Harvard Professor Stephen Jay Gould. This storehouse of priceless information within us, when tapped, has to be of great value to all, but especially to the actor. It's all there within us – all of it.

Just as there are many fields of radio wavelengths out there, allowing you to tune into the one you want, perhaps we can all tune into the universal knowledge that is in and around us, says Professor Rupert Sheldrake of Cambridge University. Many writers say they are surprised when the characters they have created on paper become independent of their creator, "come alive," and start to reveal their own lives and the direction they need to take. Many actors have the exact same experience when the character they are working on seems to take them over.

Under hypnosis, ordinary people temporarily lose inhibitions and perform extraordinary feats. The hypnotist simply gives them permission. As actors we can give ourselves permission to do what we want to do and be who we want to be.

Acting is largely a matter of consciousness–changing.

– 23 –

HOW ACTING WORKS

SEVEN NATURAL LAWS THAT MAKE ACTING POSSIBLE

A DIRECT, NON-INTELLECTUAL EXPERIENCE OF REALITY IS ESSENTIAL TO GOOD ACTING.

When you are curious about how acting works, you find yourself going to science for analogies as I have done in this and other sections of the book.

A few of the following principles have been mentioned earlier. They are brought together here to focus on some specific reasons that acting works the way it does.

1. THERE IS NO DIFFERENCE BETWEEN WHAT WE IMAGINE VIVIDLY AND WHAT IS REAL

Have you ever been in a very dark place and felt there was a menacing presence that you couldn't quite see? You sense a movement or hear a sound and you begin to sweat, get goose bumps, the hairs on your neck stand up, adrenaline shoots through you, and you are frozen. Then you turn on the light and no one is there – you only imagined it!

Nevertheless, at the time, it was real for you; the physical manifestations were very real. There is no subjective differ-ence between what we vividly imagine and what is really real. This fact is true for both the actor and the audience. Both agree to suspend reality and enter into the subjective world of the theater. There have been times when some or all members of an audience have rioted, fainted, screamed, or run out on particular performances. In the Group Theatre production of *Waiting for Lefty*, the audience stood and shouted "strike" with the actors. In Paris in 1963, dur-ing the play *Deputy* by Rolph Houchtuch, the audience start-ed a large riot.

See "New Studies Explore the Brain's Triumph Over Reality," *The New York Times*, Science Times, October 13, 1998, by Sandra Blakeslee.

2. COGNITIVE DISSONANCE.

I saw an informative documentary on the experiments of Dr. Leon Festinger and Dr. Philip Zimbardo at Stanford University. They were doing a study on cognitive disso-nance which states that we tend to believe in what we find ourselves doing, even if we believed otherwise beforehand. For instance, the member of a debating team who is asked to pick from a hat which side of the argument he will debate may pick the side of the argument with which he personal-ly disagrees. If he fights hard enough to prove this side is right, he well might begin to believe in it. Some lawyers and politicians do this regularly, as do, of course, actors. If you tell a lie often enough, you begin to believe it's the truth, in life or in acting.

This analogy from science helps us to understand why actors tend to believe in an imaginary play after rehearsing it over and over. The play becomes as real for them as their own lives. Unspoiled children do this naturally all the time.

3. SUBPERSONALITIES

We all carry within us at all times the possibility to be all people. The more facets of ourselves we can be aware of and use in our acting, the better. That means being conscious of our "dark" as well as our "light" sides. The whore, the gigolo, the saint, the devil, the nurturer, the destroyer – all the parts are within each of us. When we act, we play a part of ourselves. (See Part 3, No. 1, The Reason You Can Act.) For further information read "Embracing Ourselves," by Dr. Hal Stone (Devorss & Co.).

4. AWARENESS SHIFTING

John O. Stevens states in his book *Awareness* (Real People Press), "There are a number of zones of human awareness." We have the ability to shift our awareness from one plane or state to another. We can daydream, visualize while doing something else. We can be in a fantasy while balancing our checkbook. We can switch from ordinary life to an imagined life. We can easily experience more than one level of awareness simultaneously. We can be on stage as ourselves and be the character at the same time. We do it by intentionally or unintentionally shifting our awareness – something we constantly do in everyday life.

In the beginning rehearsals, you are more aware of yourself as actor. As rehearsals progress, you become more aware of yourself as the character. You never become completely one or the other. Perhaps you can be fully aware of only one thing at a time, but your awareness can shift back and forth so rapidly that it is as if character and actor merge. It's not uncommon for some aspects of the character to temporarily leak into your life. During the performance, your awareness keeps shifting but you want to keep it primarily on you as the character.

5. ABREACTION

Drs. Joseph Breuer and Sigmund Freud first used the name "abreaction" in Vienna in 1893. Abreaction is a term borrowed from psychoanalysis for the ability we all have to fully relive past experiences in the present. We all have experienced this many times when we have related or thought about a past tragic or comic event and strong feelings came up. It may be a song we remember, or a pet we once had. We may recall childhood friends, or a "crush," or lover. The thought of someone close to us that died in the past can evoke strong feelings in the present. This is another scientific analogy that helps explain how acting works.

6. CONDITIONED REFLEXES

The art of acting must never be reduced to the mechanical or technical. We take advantage, however, of the natural evolutionary aspect of association. You may know of Pavlov's scientific experiments with stimulating a dog's salivary glands by feeding him and ringing a bell at the same time. Later, he only needed to ring the bell to stimulate the dog's salivary glands. This led to the discovery that you could condition emotional responses. The actor learns to condition himself to respond to imaginary stimuli when he is creating a role, for example, conditioning the emotions with the playwright's words. With time, the actor develops a whole repertoire of images that can evoke a broad range of emotional responses. You can find a catalytic word, smell, sound, or taste that, like Pavlov's bell, will stimulate an emotion or feeling you need to fulfill the role being played. The actor rehearses the line of the play while evoking the stimulus; gradually, the word and the stimulus become associated and the actor need only say the lines to have the feelings come up.

7. DUAL MEMORY SYSTEMS

As stated earlier, it was reported in *The New York Times* that scientists have recently shown that we have two memory systems, one for ordinary information and one for emotionally charged information. The actor can take advantage of this second memory system for the memory of emotions she may want to use in her acting. Acting teachers have known this empirically for some time.

– 24 –

EIGHT MAJOR OBSTACLES TO GOOD ACTING AND HOW TO AVOID THEM

IF ANYONE IS AWARE YOU ARE DOING THE PROCESS, YOU ARE DOING IT WRONG.

1. EXPECTATIONS AND ANTICIPATION

Harboring expectations of how your acting "should" go is one of the main killers of good acting. Don't form pictures of the result. You can get so busy trying to make what you are doing fit the pictures that you lose spontaneity. If your work does not fit the picture, you can become negative and nervous and hurt the overall scene. Don't anticipate. (EXER-CISES: Tools #1, 4.)

2. PERFECTIONISM

The "curse of perfectionism" usually leaves you negative, unhappy, and slows you down. You can only do the best you can. Since there is no such thing as perfect, you only get frustrated and that hurts your work. (EXERCISES: Tools #1, 4.)

3. *TENSION, ANXIETY, STRESS*

These are probably the greatest thieves of natural talent because they effect your whole being, physically, mentally, psychologically, and spiritually. (EXERCISE: Tool #1.)

4. *GOING FOR RESULTS RATHER THAN CAUSES*

It's all right to go for what causes the particular result you want, but never for the results directly. (EXERCISES: Tools #4, 5.)

5. *COMPARING*

To compare, especially while working, how the acting you are now doing stacks up with previous work pulls you away and weakens the present acting work. Comparing yourself or your acting with others uses up vital energy. (EXERCISE: Tool #1.)

6. THE MILLISECOND FILTER

Many people rescued from drowning report that their whole life seemed to flash before their eyes. Unfortunately, when many an actor is about to say his or her first line, all the actor's fears, insecurities, and negativity can flash through his brain in a millisecond and filter out the actor's full talent. (EXERCISES: As a distraction from tension, concentrate on any or all tools.)

7. BEING SUBJECTIVE AND OBJECTIVE AT THE SAME TIME

Some actors try to act and "watch" themselves act at the same time, to be on the stage and in the audience simultaneously. This puts a damper on your acting, like putting a blanket over your head. Trying to be fully in two places at the same time, you cancel out and are nowhere. (EXERCISE: Tool #1.)

8. LISTENING TO YOURSELF AS YOU SPEAK

Like "watching" yourself on stage, whenever you "hear" yourself, know, positively, that you are not doing your best work. Get back to your character's needs or anything you can concentrate on within the play or character or your partners. (EXERCISES: Tools #1 through 13, as a distraction from listening to the words of the play.)

25

NINE COMMON TYPES OF ACTORS AND WHAT YOU CAN LEARN TO AVOID FROM THEM

ACTING IS NOT AN INTELLECTUAL CONCEPT DISTINCT FROM NATURE.

NOTE: Be aware that these "types" frequently come in combinations.

1. THE HEAD ACTOR

This type of actor thinks he can act with his mind alone. He analyzes the character and then tries to let the audience know that he "understands" the character.

Understand the character with your heart, not just your head. Acting at its best is a holistic, visceral, multi-dimensional experience for the actor and the audience. When I first started to teach, some of my students had previously studied with teachers who encouraged analytical, intellectual work. They would submit, unasked for, extremely well-written papers that thoroughly analyzed their characters. I would think, "This is going to be great." Then when they did their scene, there were only empty shells, talking heads with no flesh on the bones of their characters.

Later, at the "Writers–Directors" unit of the Actors Studio, I saw famous playwrights act in their own plays and fail miserably. I thought, "Who should understand the character better than the person who created him?" A few well-respected critics also acted in that unit and their acting was worse. But in their reviews, their analyses of plays and characters would be brilliant. It became apparent to me that this kind of "head" work is not what makes a good actor. I am not against intelligent actors; on the contrary. I am for a balance. My ideal actor could have the brains of a genius and the emotions of a young child or baby. Einstein said, "Brilliance is nothing more than childhood revisited at will."

2. ACTORS WITH INGRAINED BAD ACTING HABITS

Bad habits often get ingrained when someone performs with a group in front of an audience before learning to act. With no one to guide him or her properly, the actor begins to imitate acting. The more an untrained person acts for poor directors, and the bigger the parts, the deeper the habits get ingrained and the more difficult they are to erase.

Another way to acquire bad acting habits is to work with bad acting teachers who know neither how to prevent bad habits nor how to correct them (see the list of types of acting teachers below – Part 3, #5).

3. THE SLICK ACTOR

The slick actor learns all the "tricks" of acting and usually

just gets slicker and shallower the more he acts. There is little or no heart in his acting. He may learn the craft and
skills of acting, but leaves the human element out.

4. THE VOICE ACTOR.

This type of actor "sings" his lines. Such actors are often
found doing classical material, where the writing is heightened and is called "style." The voices, manners, and costumes try to capture this "style." There are actors who do
this type of acting very well and there are others who just
imitate it badly. Some actors "sing" or use "special" voices –
in both classical and contemporary plays – that are just
phony. Shakespeare said they "mouth" the words (*Hamlet*,
Act III, Scene 2). When asked on David Frost's show what
he would do differently if he had to do it over, Sir John
Gielgud (in his eighties) said, "I would not sing my lines."

5. THE CLOWN

The "clown" actor thinks he or she has to "help" the play by
making faces, grimacing, and playing to the audience. This
actor gives the audience signals: "Get ready to laugh – this
is funny." Some members of the audience, trained by TV,
bad comics, and canned laughter, even respond. There are
quality laughs and there are cheap laughs. Shakespeare
obviously abhorred this kind of actor and audience. In his
"advice to the players," he talks about bad clowning and
barren spectators who laugh at it. He says to the comic

actors, "That's villainous and shows a most pitiful ambition in the fool that uses it." (See "Playing Comedy" Part 2, No. 2.)

6. THE PERSONALITY ACTOR

These people are more often seen in film than on stage. They can become famous and rich, but are rarely acclaimed for their acting. A rock singer or a sports personality that turns to acting can fit this category. Sometimes they get better with experience, and can do well if they are careful to stay with roles close to their own personalities, but they are rarely respected for their acting.

7. THE "PATTERNS" ACTOR

These actors memorize their lines in a comfortable pattern, then repeat this pattern every time they say the lines, down to the last emphasis and rhythm. The scenery could fall down or their partner drop dead, but they go on with their pattern as if nothing happened. It has little to do with the changes within them or their fellow actors. To the audience, they sound rehearsed and mismatched. In Shakespeare's "Advice," he said, "Suit the action to the word, the word to the action." This piece of advice is lost to the patterns actor (See Tools #4, 6, 7).

8. THE IMAGINATION ACTOR

Acting is making the imaginary real. There are some actors who make the imaginary – well, imaginary. Now, imagination is an essential ingredient for any artist. But just as an imaginary meal is not very nourishing or life- sustaining, neither is an actor who works only in the imagination. We are talking about the actor who is all pretense and imitation and who leaves out anything real or authentic. There are actors who want to leave out the essential ingredient of the "visceral." These actors are afraid to reveal their humanity so they imitate reality. Through the diligent practice of "acting tools," each actor can find the specific blend of what is real and what is ideal, dealing with what is actual while always looking for something ideal.

9. THE GENERAL ENERGY ACTOR

This actor uses general energy in place of specific feeling. They can seem exciting, but their acting is frenetic, empty, and easily forgettable.

26

SEVEN MAJOR TYPES OF ACTING TEACHERS TO AVOID

(AND ONE YOU MAY WANT TO EMBRACE)

A more practical name for talent may be "the ability to reveal" – to reveal oneself, all you can be, and the full humanness within.

You can encounter at least eight major types of acting teachers. (Again, they often come in combinations.) Some examples are:

1. THE "CRITIC" TYPE OF TEACHER

The "critic" type doesn't really know how to teach you to act – only how to criticize. You often think, because they can be sharp and knowing and hard on you, that they will somehow embarrass you into becoming an actor. They play on your feelings of inadequacy because they need to feel superior. They can be popular but, in the long run, most often do more harm than good.

2. THE "DIRECTOR" TYPE OF TEACHER

The "director" type can't really teach you to act – so they direct you. This type of teacher can be very popular because the teacher does all the work for you. He or she often feels you don't know anything and doesn't have the patience to guide you toward finding and owning skills for yourself. This type of teacher can make your work look good – temporarily. The problem is, without this teacher you are lost. The "director" never taught you to act, and you have to start from scratch every time.

3. THE "GURU" TYPE OF TEACHER

This teacher needs the class more than the class needs him. The gurus need admirers to make them feel good, to compensate for not making it themselves. This type of teacher loves you and you love him or her back, but you don't really learn to act.

4. THE "ACTOR" (OR FRUSTRATED ACTOR) TYPE OF TEACHER

The class is a substitute for the acting jobs this type of teacher can't get. He or she competes with the students and you had better not be better than he is. This kind of teacher frequently demonstrates all the parts, often badly, and wants you to imitate him (God forbid!).

5. THE "PLAYWRIGHT" TYPE OF TEACHER

They think that if you understand the script you will auto-matically be able to act it. They don't teach you to act; they teach you how to analyze the text. If understanding alone were the answer, then the writer of the play or the theater critic would be the best actor. It just ain't so! Understanding and interpreting the script is vital but this is the beginning for the actor, not the end.

6. THE "INTELLECTUAL" TYPE OF TEACHER

Generally, this teacher learned about acting from an intel-lectual who learned from an intellectual. It's all very neat and logical and theoretical, but has little to do with the real world of the theatre.

7. THE IMPROVISATIONAL TEACHER

There are instructors who rely too heavily on improvisation as their main technique for teaching acting. Their students often love it. They don't have to learn lines and it can be a lot of fun, like charades. It feels like instant acting. The major problem with too much improvisation is that it can easily make for undisciplined and sloppy acting habits. I have had students who had worked this way for a long time before I met them, and they know little or nothing about how to approach a scene that is structured in any way.

Improvisation can be a good tool for general looseness where needed. It can be good for solving specific problems; for instance, to bring reality to an important event mentioned in the script but never written out. Improvisation can be used to break the ice between actors. Sometimes, you are asked to improvise while auditioning (See the Big Three Exercise, Tool #8).

Improvisation is a very good tool if used properly and sparingly, but not relied on exclusively. The same can be true of sloppy presentational or street theater. Some talented teachers and actors can successfully merge improvisation with meaningful structure.

8. THE IDEAL TEACHER

He or she has experienced it all personally, first hand, and has the ability and the eagerness to pass it on to whomever is interested. This teacher has no bitterness about not making it big in the theatre. His standards are high, but he is patient and totally supportive. This teacher knows you have it all within you and that his job is to coax it out of you rather than to try to push something in. He has enthusiasm, love, and respect for the profession of acting and for the students. This teacher is more interested in how much you learn than in how popular he is. As a teacher he is clear and practical and the people he works with can eventually perform any style of material in any media with confidence. He knows that there is acting that imitates nature but teaches a kind of acting that is nature. This teacher cleared up most of his personal problems and does not project them onto the students in various forms. The ideal teacher does not give you a fish to feed you for one meal but teaches you how to fish for yourself and so feeds you for a lifetime. His teaching is in harmony with the laws of nature and he respects you as an organic whole person.

Once, a boy playing outside a wall heard constant hammering from the other side. Curious, he climbed the wall. He saw a man with a mallet and chisel. "Hey," he shouted, "why are you hitting that stone?" Michelangelo looked up and said, "there's a man named David trapped inside this stone and I want to set him free."

The ideal teacher can feel like a sculptor chipping away what students don't need to get to the authentic actor inside. At other times he feels like a gardener nurturing his pupils to grow and blossom.

– 27 –

BECOMING MAGNETIC

*THERE IS AN INDEFINABLE QUALITY THAT COMES
INTO YOUR ACTING
FROM THE WAY YOU LIVE YOUR LIFE.*

Dr. Rupert Sheldrake, a scientist at Cambridge University, has written that "every organism has a field like a magnet." This is another analogy from science that can inform the actor. You, no doubt, have heard of people and performers who have magnetic personalities; maybe you know some-one like this. These people usually believe in themselves; they are positive and feel powerful. They have enthusiasm and confidence. They smile a great deal and are dynamic. "Plastic people" have no magnetism. Don't be a plastic actor.

EXERCISE

For Developing Magnetism and Charisma

Stand facing a partner, about ten feet apart. Raise one foot a few inches above the ground and strike it down flatly on the ground. The part of the body that has kept in touch with the earth are the feet, the supporting base of all activ-ities, including acting. To complete an electric circuit you must have ground. This explains why birds on a highly charged electric wire don't get electrocuted; they are not connected to the ground. Let the energy rise up your legs from the ground and through your whole body. Make a primitive growling sound as you thrust out your arms. Alternate feet. Soon you should feel charged with positive currents around you as you become one with the universal force in the universe. Become a dynamo and let magnetic energy stream through your eyes, hands, toes, pelvis – your whole body. Align your specific magnetic energy and let it stream toward your partner. As you may know, the ends of a magnet are called poles and are either positive or nega- tive. The poles can either attract or repel. Opposite poles attract, poles that are alike repel. The partners use a strong attracting force. One is negative and the other is positive. They very slowly move toward each other. They pass in the center slightly brushing shoulders; this is the strongest point. They proceed to the opposite side; now being back to back, they keep moving as they sense the magnetism with their backs until they turn around and face each other again. Next, they recharge; this time using strong negative repelling energy. Both have like poles. They move toward each other brushing shoulders and again feeling the force with their backs as they move away. The next time they move, they decide independently if they are going to use attracting or repelling energy. After trying many variations, they can, when they meet in the center, do a magnetic "dance" around each other varying the attraction and repul- sion at will. If you have a group, they can then join anoth- er couple, then that group joins another group until every- one is moving around each other like so many atoms. They can be aware and respond to each other's positive and neg- ative fields. This exercise can be done alone, with a partner, or with a group. Different from above, when done alone, practice magnetizing yourself with energy at will as outlined above without using a partner, like a magnet standing alone.

EXERCISE

Magnetizing an Audience

Webster tells us that "induction" is a "process by which an object having magnetic properties produces similar properties in a nearby object, usually without direct contact." Put a nail near a magnet without touching it directly. That nail will, by induction, become a magnet itself and can induce magnetism into another nail without touching it and on and on from nail to nail, depending on the power of the original magnet. In other words, without direct contact, the magnetism can pass from object to object. In acting terms, I define induction as that ability the actor has to align his own inner energy into a magnetic force that then is induced unconsciously, into an audience. An audience loves to be stimulated by a performer. You work to own this power. You must never use it consciously or intentionally toward an audience when you are performing as an actor in a straight play.

Experiment with having a circle of people facing in the same direction. One person turns to face the person now in front of her and, without touching, induces strong magnetic energy into that person as described above. When that person feels the energy, he turns and induces magnetism into the next person, and so on around the circle, continuing until fully charged. When someone turns away from you, continue to induce the magnetism through their back,

strengthening the force until the whole circle is one powerful magnet. The circle can then break into a line, ready to
magnetize a whole audience in ensemble. If you don't have
a group to work with, you can work with a partner or work
alone using the above principles.

Induction is a means, not an end in itself. Its purpose is
to make you more dynamic as an actor and to indirectly
stimulate the audience. This quality could, by following the
tools outlined in this book, become something you personally own for life.

Marilyn Monroe was a classmate of mine when I studied with Lee Strasberg. After class, we would all go to Child's
Restaurant on 47th & Broadway in Manhattan. Marilyn
wore no make-up at all and would dress very simply in low
heels, with a scarf covering her blonde hair. No one paid
attention to her. She blended in with everyone else. Once
when we were talking about this magnetism she said,
"Watch!" Whatever she did, she turned it on and everyone
we passed, man, woman, and child, reacted to her.

We can all learn to switch on this magnetism with practice, and yes, sexual energy is involved.

To have strong magnetism, you need good health and
energy. Don't dissipate; have a healthy diet and exercise.

NOTE

When you are involved with actors whose way of working
happens to be the same or similar to yours, that's gravy. If
not, it's not a big problem. Don't try to convert them. It will
only end up hurting your work because you will be con-

centrating on them; besides, they are likely to resent it. If an actor or director speaks a different "acting language," try to get their true meaning by asking specific questions for clarity, and translate it into your own process of working. Ask yourself, "What tool do I have that will give them the result they want?"

You have the tools now to be a complete actor!

AFTERWORD

STUDENT What happens when an artist is being creative:

TEACHER: When an artist is being creative, impulse over-rides the rational. All fear, anxiety, negativity drop away and a clear channel opens to what you are focused on in the present moment.

STUDENT: How do you become a great actor?

TEACHER: By choosing the right tools at the right time.

STUDENT: How do you know how to choose the right tools?

TEACHER: By experience.

STUDENT: How do you get experience?

TEACHER: You must risk choosing the wrong tools until you learn to choose the right tools at the right time.

> Fear of failure can make us impotent.
> If a thing is worth doing –
> It's worth the risk of doing it "badly."

Acting is a series of connected processes. Each tool is an individual process leading to the whole Process of acting.

Acting is too complex to have a simple, all-inclusive definition. Nevertheless, for beginning work, I use: "Acting is making the impersonal (script), personal." For the next stage,

I use: "Acting is making the imaginary (script), real." The final, important step is: "Acting is making the internal (work), external."

The practice of acting changes your life, as every actor I have worked with will affirm. The brain controls our behavior and our behavior changes the circuitry of our brain.

(See *Inside the Brain* by Robert Koutlak.) Acting affects our whole way of being.

Because of the introspective nature of acting, we must never forget that there is a higher purpose to theater. Theater reveals life in all its many aspects. Theater can help us understand ourselves, others, and the world around us by exposing both the greatness and the foibles of the human condition and, hopefully will lead to a more meaningful and productive life for us and for our audiences.

Most of the tools presented for acting can be used to enhance your life. Your life is a play that is constantly being written. The most tragic ending would be to die with all the music in you still unplayed. You might as well write a happy ending for yourself.

I've had a great and rewarding life in the theater, and if it's your bliss, I hope you will follow it too. Thank you!

YES!
THE GHOST OF JERRY BUNDLER
HAUNTS ME STILL!
WATCH OUT!
HE MAY GET YOU!

LIST OF EXERCISES

TOOL #1: Neutralizing the Self; Relaxation
  Mind, psyche, spirit, body
  Relaxed Rehearsal

TOOL #2: Actualizing the Self; Sensory Reliving
  Sensory Reliving
  Touch
  Sound
  Smell Awareness
  Taste
  Seeing
  Sensing a Meaningful Object
  Sensory Rehearsing

TOOL #3: Actualizing the Self; Physical Reliving
  The Imaginary Body
  Advanced Scene Work
  Physical Reliving with Rehearsal

TOOL #4; Neutralizing the Script in Order to Actualize it More Fully
  Neutralizing the Script

TOOL #5: Actualizing the Script; Emotional Reliving
   Emotional Reliving
   Life History

TOOL #6: Neutralizing and Actualizing Your Acting Partners
   Neutralizing Your Acting Partners
   Personalization
   Intimacy
   Weapons

TOOL #7: The Three "R's" of Acting: Receive–React–Respond
   Juxtapose Real & Imaginary
   Give and Take

TOOL #8: The Big Three: Needs–Obstacles–Strategy
   Needs
   Obstacles
   Actions and Strategy
   Improvisation

TOOL #9: Breaking Down and Memorizing the Script
   Script Breakdown
   Moments

TOOL #10: Preparation
   Preparation for getting to the condition the character is
   in before performing

PART 2

1. Stepping into Character
Animal Substitution

2. Notes on Playing Comedy

3. Acting the Classics (Style and Costume)
Paintings

4. The Business of Show Business

PART 3

6. Developing Magnetism and Charisma
Magnetizing an Audience

INDEX

THE ACTOR AND THE TEXT
by Cicely Berry

As voice director of the Royal Shakespeare Company, Cicely Berry has worked with actors such as Jeremy Irons, Derek Jacobi, Jonathan Pryce, Sinead Cusack and Antony Sher. *The Actor and The Text* brings Ms. Berry's methods of applying vocal production skills within a text to the general public.

While this book focuses primarily on speaking Shakespeare, Ms. Berry also includes the speaking of some modern playwrights, such as Edward Bond.

As Ms. Berry describes her own volume in the introduction:

" ... this book is not simply about making the voice sound more interesting. It is about getting inside the words we use ...It is about making the language organic, so that the words act as a spur to the sound ..."

paper•ISBN 1-155783-138-6

APPLAUSE

CREATING A CHARACTER:
A Physical Approach to Acting
by Moni Yakim with Muriel Broadman

"Moni Yakim's techniques to attain characterization have been outstandingly successful in bringing out of his students emotional depth to enrich whatever they do on stage. [He] is an inspired teacher. His ideas and practices, which the book details, make it required reading for every serious student of the theatre."

—from the foreword by Stella Adler

"So often actors forget that there are bodies attached to their character's heads. Through Moni Yakim's technique I learned to develop the physical life of a character, lifting the character off the page and into reality."

—Patti Lupone

"Moni Yakim's teaching awakens the actor's senses and tunes the actor's physicality to a degree of self-expression beyond the merely naturalistic and into the larger realms of imagination and poetry."

—Kevin Kline

paper • ISBN: 1-55783-161-0

APPLAUSE

STANISLAVSKI REVEALED
by Sonia Moore

Other than Stanislavski's own published work, the most widely read interpretation of his techniques remains Sonia Moore's pioneering study, The Stanislavski System. Sonia Moore is on the frontier again now as she reveals the subtle tissue of ideas behind what Stanislavski regarded as his "major breakthrough," the Method of Physical Actions. Moore has devoted the last decade in her world-famous studio to an investigation of Stanislavski's final technique. The result is the first detailed discussion of Moore's own theory of psychophysical unity which she has based on her intensive practical meditation on Stanislavski's consummate conclusions about acting.

Demolishing the popular notion that his methods depend on private—self-centered—expression, Moore now reveals Stanislavski as the advocate of deliberate, controlled, conscious technique—internal and external at the same time—a technique that makes tremendous demands on actors but that rewards them with the priceless gift of creative life.

paper • ISBN: 1-55783-103-3

MONOLOGUE WORKSHOP

From Search to Discovery
in Audition and Performance

by Jack Poggi

To those for whom the monologue has always been synonymous with terror, *The Monologue Workshop* will prove an indispensable ally. Jack Poggi's new book answers the long-felt need among actors for top-notch guidance in finding, rehearsing and performing monologues. For those who find themselves groping for speech just hours before their "big break," this book is their guide to salvation.

The Monologue Workshop supplies the tools to discover new pieces before they become over-familiar, excavate older material that has been neglected, and adapt material from non-dramatic sources (novels, short stories, letters, diaries, autobiographies, even newspaper columns). There are also chapters on writing original monologues and creating solo performances in the style of Lily Tomlin and Eric Bogosian.

Besides the wealth of practical advice he offers, Poggi transforms the monologue experience from a terrifying ordeal into an exhilarating opportunity. Jack Poggi, as many working actors will attest, is the actor's partner in a process they had always thought was without one.

paper•ISBN 1-55783-031-2 • $12.95